The Realities of Comp

CU00656204

The Realities of Completing a PhD gives a balanced and evidence-based view of the realities of PhD life. Full of practical tips and including a checklist to complete before sending an application, the book helps prospective PhD students prepare for the realities of taking on a PhD from an informed basis and offers guidance on submitting a well-planned application.

This is the first book of its kind to bring together a range of international data that helps to paint a more balanced picture of the PhD process. The book outlines different types of PhD, how to select a topic for a PhD, how to write a robust research proposal and application, and the realities of PhD study in relation to student wellbeing, social commitments and employment prospects. By considering the issues raised in this book, students are less likely to be overwhelmed by the PhD process, and better equipped to complete their award.

The book will be invaluable for potential doctoral students as well as those already embarking on a PhD. It will also enable university mentors and supervisors to consider how the application phase is key to managing student expectations, and how they can further promote a healthy and productive PhD experience.

Nicholas Rowe is a trans-disciplinary educationalist, with interests in scientific communication and academic/professional development. A dual fellow of the UK Higher Education Academy and the Society for Education and Training, he worked as a full-time lecturer in the UK and did his PhD in education in Finland.

Routledge Research in Education

This series aims to present the latest research from right across the field of education. It is not confined to any particular area or school of thought and seeks to provide coverage of a broad range of topics, theories and issues from around the world. Recent titles in the series include:

Curriculum and the Generation of Utopia
Interrogating the Current State of Critical Curriculum Theory
João M. Paraskeva

Sport, Physical Education, and Social Justice
Religious, Sociological, Psychological, and Capability Perspectives
Edited by Nick J. Watson, Grant Jarvie and Andrew Parker

Quality and Equity in Education
Revisiting Theory and Research on Educational Effectiveness and Improvement
Leonidas Kyriakides, Bert P. M. Creemers, Anastasia Panayiotou, & Evi Charalambous

Creative Learning in Digital and Virtual Environments
Opportunities and Challenges of Technology-Enabled Learning and Creativity
Edited by Vlad P. Glăveanu, Ingunn Johanne Ness, and Constance de Saint Laurent

Reconceptualizing the Role of Critical Dialogue in American Classrooms
Promoting Equity through Dialogic Education
Edited by Amanda Kibler, Guadalupe Valdés and Aída Walqui

The Realities of Completing a PhD
How to Plan for Success
Nicholas Rowe

For a complete list of titles in this series, please visit www.routledge.com/Routledge-Research-in-Education/book-series/SE0393

The Realities of Completing a PhD

How to Plan for Success

Nicholas Rowe

Routledge
Taylor & Francis Group

LONDON AND NEW YORK

First published 2021
by Routledge
2 Park Square, Milton Park, Abingdon, Oxon OX14 4RN

and by Routledge
52 Vanderbilt Avenue, New York, NY 10017

Routledge is an imprint of the Taylor & Francis Group, an informa business

© 2021 Nicholas Rowe

British Library Cataloguing-in-Publication Data
A catalogue record for this book is available from the British Library

Library of Congress Cataloging-in-Publication Data
A catalog record has been requested for this book

ISBN: 978-0-367-67762-6 (hbk)
ISBN: 978-0-367-67764-0 (pbk)
ISBN: 978-1-003-13271-4 (ebk)

Typeset in Times New Roman
by SPi Global, India

This book is dedicated to all those past, present and future PhDs who have worked their way through the PhD system, often relying on pure grit, determination and resilience. Equally, it acknowledges all of those who have not reached the finish line (possibly through no fault of their own), and whose voices are often not heard. Hopefully, this portrayal of the realities of doing a PhD and how best to approach the process will help university staff understand the wider PhD student experience, and enable future PhD students to walk into their programmes better prepared and ready to face the challenges ahead.

Contents

List of illustrations

Figures

Tables

Glossary

ABD (All But Dissertation)   A term sometimes used to indicate that someone has completed their PhD coursework, but has not gone on to complete the award (i.e. the dissertation and examination).

Academic discipline   An academic discipline is the main field you wish to study in. It is divided into sub-disciplines that define a particular area, and branches of the sub-discipline that define specific areas of approach or interest.

Bachelor's degree   A first-level degree examined at level 6 on the European Qualifications Framework (EQF). A bachelor's degree with honours (Hons) usually contains a larger volume of material, a higher standard of study or both, rather than an ordinary bachelor's degree. It often has a research element.

Dissertation (see Thesis)   In Europe, the term dissertation is often used interchangeably with thesis but reflects a broader post-graduate research project. In the US a thesis is often used to describe master's-level work, and the term dissertation is used for doctoral work.

Doctorate   A qualification that awards a doctoral degree examined at level 8 on the European Qualifications Framework (EQF). It is seen as a terminal degree and is the highest-level award a university can bestow.

Master's degree   A second-level degree examined at level 7 on the European Qualifications Framework (EQF). It may also be referred to as a graduate degree.

Monograph thesis   A monograph thesis presents a candidate's overall research in one document for evaluation for a doctoral award.

New route/integrated PhD   A four-year programme consisting of a one-year research master's degree (MRes), followed by a three-year PhD.

PhD   Doctor of Philosophy

PhD by prior publication/portfolio   An award based on publications that are already in the public domain, with a shorter introductory thesis and an oral defense.

PhD by publication   A PhD by publication (also known as a compilation thesis) is where the candidate publishes 3–5 articles in peer reviewed journals, then produces a summary thesis for examination.

Professional doctorate   A professional doctorate is a work-based degree, aimed at developing skills, expertise and knowledge to advance practice within a specific profession. This involves the creation and interpretation of new knowledge and practice, and the development of new ideas, methods or approaches.

Research degree   A research degree (e.g. PhD/MPhil) is based on an independent research project, as opposed to a programme of assessed coursework. There may be mandatory courses/credits that you have to complete, but these are not the focus of the awarded degree.

Thesis (see Dissertation)   In Europe, the term thesis is often used interchangeably with dissertation and refers firstly to a formal statement or theory proposed by the candidate, and secondly to the piece of work that lays out the detail and argument of their proposal.

Under-employment   Having a job that is less than full time and inadequate in regard to using the actual training an employee has or failing to meet reasonable economic needs.

Undergraduate degree   A first-level degree examined at level 6 on the European Qualifications Framework (EQF).

Viva/viva-voce   An oral examination where you give a verbal defense of your thesis. Also known as your doctoral defense.

Introduction

A PhD is a unique and individual undertaking, entirely unlike any other academic course you will have done before. Universities accept only those with high potential to complete, but their success is not guaranteed. Globally, only 1.1% of 25- to 64-year-olds have a doctoral level education (Hutt 2019), and a doctorate is generally seen as the highest academic achievement you can obtain. However, in the US, despite producing the highest number of doctorates, figures show that only slightly more than 50% of those who take on a PhD actually graduate (Lani 2020). Even if you follow data all the way back to the 1950s, the average reported completion rate has been only 61%. But this is not just a US phenomenon, and low figures are quoted for Europe (66%: European University Association 2019) and the UK (70%: Jump 2013). Pinning down realistic and representative data is, however, difficult. As an example, in Australia some figures quote 70% to 80% of students completing their PhDs (ANU 2019), but other sources from mainstream educational media quoting government data (Australian Government 2020) show that from 2010 to 2016, the national completion rate for master's/PhD programmes was a shocking 14.9% (Khan 2018). So, it is clear that until more consistent and reliable data becomes available, then researchers, institutions and potential PhD students will find predicting the chances of PhD success a difficult undertaking.

Doing a PhD is not expected to be plain sailing, but above the intellectual challenges students face, the high-level stress and anxiety postgraduate students experience is 10 times that seen in the general population (Bira et al. 2019). Furthermore, there is a very low chance that they will gain employment at a university on a full-time contract (European Science Foundation 2017), despite having such a high-level and closely aligned qualification.

However, there are also many who complete their PhD studies on time, having had a wonderful and supported experience, and who also go on to secure well-paid employment. For example, Harvard Law School has a graduation rate of 98% (Ehrenberg & Kuh 2011); Imperial College London, 90% (Jump 2010); etc. But the balance between these groups is not even, and the little available evidence we have shows that thousands of students across different institutions and countries experience a disassociation with what they had hoped their PhD journey would be like, and the realities that they face once committed.

The available statistics show that completion rates have remained consistently low over the last few decades, and universities seem to have been thinking of PhD completion rates as something inherent to the study process. However, two important factors are worth noting here.

First, while a PhD is inherently demanding and academically challenging, *all* of those accepted onto programmes have been pre-screened in terms of their academic ability and research potential. Furthermore, intense competition for places and relatively low acceptance rates infer that only those with the greatest potential are selected. Yet despite being 'the best of the best', many of those who start do not finish, and this involves vast numbers of students every year. Given the resources committed by institutions, funders and the students themselves to doing a PhD, the rate of 'dropout' is highly important, and given the pre-screening and selection processes involved, dropout is likely to be a result of the PhD process, and not individually student-driven.

Second, damagingly high rates of negative mental health and wellbeing among PhD students (and academic staff in general) are shown in a range of international studies, yet universities seem to have adopted a position of accepting issues of wellbeing as something primarily beyond their control, a consequence of high-level academic performance, and something that needs to be managed (for example, by post-hoc counselling). Elements such as stress, anxiety, depression, isolation and suicidal thoughts are both high and commonly reported across the international literature, and given the rise in doctoral enrolment, the numbers of those affected are similarly likely to involve large numbers of students every year. However, little accessible information is available for staff or students to knowledgably prepare for PhD study, and the PhD experience remains relatively unchanged from one generation of scholars to the next.

This book collates statistical, personal and institutional perspectives and shows that expanding the support prospective students get to prepare for their PhD study can have a significant impact on the stress, dissatisfaction and dropout related to PhD programmes. Furthermore, graduating students will have better chances of aligning their employment goals with their qualification, and so make their PhD process more efficient and rewarding.

Aims of this book

This book serves two purposes and is essentially a 'book of two halves'. In Part 1, the realities of doing a PhD are made clear using best available evidence to illustrate the general PhD student situation in regard to admission, completion, experience and wellbeing. While it is acknowledged that there are many institutions that achieve good graduation rates, the published data of large-scale studies and reports shows that vast numbers of students internationally fail to complete their PhD, despite having already been assessed by their universities as being academically able and having the potential to develop the skills and knowledge necessary to complete their research journey. Furthermore, with no evidence of a pre-disposition to mental illness, PhD students suffer in terms of their mental health and wellbeing, struggle financially and incur high levels of education-related debt, and often have complex personal circumstances where they juggle their work, life and social commitments. It is envisaged that these specific factors cause them to drop out and experience reduced wellbeing and outcomes. To illustrate the issues involved, more personal student considerations are discussed regarding the time needed to study, maintaining family and social commitments, financial issues, international study and special needs requirements. Thus, the first 'half' of this book lays out *the realities of completing a PhD* on both general and personal levels, bringing together published data from a range of countries and sources. While these issues are perhaps discouraging, having an awareness of them will help to prepare potential PhD students for what lies ahead, and help universities re-evaluate the PhD student experience to improve their outcomes. To this end, some points for consideration are offered for both students and universities/institutions.

Moving forward, Part 2 of this book is student-focused on the PhD application and preparing for PhD study. While there are lots of books that address how students can 'survive' their PhD, this book helps potential students make an informed decision as to whether they are well positioned to take on a PhD in the first place, and what to consider when applying for a study position. Taking this approach will allow students to be better prepared for their PhD journey, and so enhance their chances of completion. Furthermore, making informed choices that go beyond just 'doing a PhD' are likely to encourage the development of skills and knowledge that will be more readily welcomed in a range of work settings once they graduate.

While this book has been written as a solo project, these aims are concurrent with the envisaged outcomes (p. 24) of the RoRI Working Paper "21st Century PhDs" (Hancock et al. 2019), which is another indicator that the access, experiences and outcomes of doctoral study are of international interest. Particularly, they reiterate the need for meaningful data to help inform decisions, as well as action by institutions and bodies to develop the PhD process.

To quote a vernacular military saying: "Prior preparation and planning prevents piss-poor performance". In terms of measures of completion, wellbeing, employment and return on investment, the current PhD system has severe drawbacks, but students can minimize their impact with careful pre-emption and planning for what lies ahead.

Source data and PhD terminology

Among the academic literature, there is very little research and data that shows how PhD students perfom, beyond fairly narrow studies of particular programmes and groups. As this book addresses a globally widespread audience, the sources used tend to represent data reported by government institutions and the popular/professional press, as opposed to adopting a purely academic focus on peer-reviewed literature (which is not currently available in sufficient quantity). The sources used are listed at the end of the book.

As a further point, the term 'PhD' is used throught the book as a familiar reference to include all doctoral-level degrees, although the differences between degree types is fully covered in the Glossary and the main text. A similar approach has been used in recent policy studies.

Part 1

The realities of doing a PhD

Issues affecting student dropout, completion, employment and wellbeing

1   What is a PhD and why do one?

Unlike the taught (with or without research) programmes of bachelor's and master's degrees, a PhD or other doctoral award is awarded to students who complete an original thesis that offers a significant new contribution to their field of knowledge. It is commonly seen as being the highest award that may be conferred by a university.

Although many PhD programmes have a mandatory study requirement (where you have to complete a certain amount of study units or credits), the main element of a PhD is your final thesis or dissertation, based on independent research. Universities usually provide taught courses to students to give them the skills and knowledge that will help them in their research, but the main focus is on accessing and completing study units, and not achieving a high grade. Although some countries grade a final thesis (for example, Finland), most simply award a PASS or FAIL judgement based on the thesis evaluation and meeting programme and examination panel requirements – either you get it, or you don't.

In a PhD, you produce high-level original research of your own, so being a good independent researcher is far more important than simply being a good student. This aspect is examined even before you are enrolled on a programme, and you will be expected to have either formulated your own specific research plan (perhaps investigating a new topic or problem in your field), or to demonstrate your ability or potential to investigate part of an existing project. Depending on your field and the institution you apply to, your chances of acceptance depend on the number of places available and also on the quality of the other applications they receive. A recent US study (American Psychological Association 2016) showed acceptance rates of between 6% and 31% across subfields, with an overall acceptance rate of 13%. Many institutions now require that you find a potential supervisor *prior* to applying, so as well as locating them and establishing contact, you will have to convince them of the benefit of your proposed research, and also of your potential to see it through. Having a good bachelor's or master's degree classification in a related field is only one element of this (many of those competing for the same position will have similar or better qualifications), so your research proposal is of vital importance. If you do not have a clear idea of what you want to do, why it is important and how you aim to do it, you are unlikely to be accepted. Perhaps worse, if you start a PhD without this initial framework in place, you are going to find the PhD process exceptionally challenging.

The data universities publish on PhD performance tends to focus on the numbers of doctorates they award, and there is very little data that shows how many people drop out or fail to complete. As an indicator of this, the term 'ABD' (*all but dissertation*) has now become commonplace on CVs where people show that they have completed their PhD-level coursework but have not gone on to complete the award (i.e. complete an examined thesis), and are therefore not entitled to the title of 'doctor' or to claim a doctoral degree. So being accepted and doing well on coursework will not be enough to achieve a PhD. Recognizing a PhD for what it is (the independent completion of an original thesis that offers a significant new contribution to the field of knowledge), and not simply as a high-level study degree, is the first

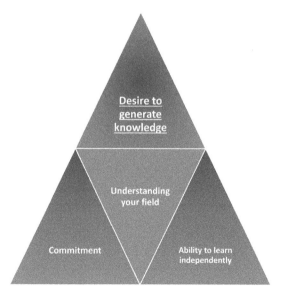

Figure 1.1 Required traits that motivate a good PhD application.

thing you need to be aware of *before* thinking of making a PhD application (see Figure 1.1 for the traits that motivate a good PhD application).

Why do a PhD?

Everyone has their own idea of why they want to do a PhD. However, being able to describe your motivations for doing a PhD to yourself and others will not only influence your chances of being accepted onto a programme, but also improve your chances of completing it and enjoying your overall PhD experience.

Published data shows that a PhD is an earned research degree that takes years to complete, often at considerable financial and personal sacrifice – there are no shortcuts or easy ways to complete it. The return for your commitment and effort is firstly the award of a degree that acknowledges your achievement. But secondly, the research and study you do should also have concrete outcomes in terms of what it does for you (e.g. in career and life enhancement), and what it does for others (scientific advancement, societal development, etc.). These two things are not mutually exclusive, and it is not unreasonable to expect some personal reward for your efforts. But the strongest PhD students tend to be driven by their work, and not because they want to 'become a doctor'. All too often PhD aspirants say '*I want to do a PhD*', but without a clearly thought-out research plan (or at least a comprehensive idea of one), this sort of statement says you are looking at a PhD mainly as a credential and have not really thought about what a PhD is or what you will have to do to *earn* the degree. Research is a field where planning and vision are vital, so being able to clearly describe *why* you want to do a PhD will be a good indicator as to whether you will be able to identify a specific topic to examine, ask the right questions during your research, analyse the answers and draw the right conclusions (that's research!). Simply 'wanting to do a PhD' is not a good enough reason to apply for a PhD position.

How skilled and 'expert' do I have to be before I apply?

You are not expected to have all the answers and skills when you start your PhD programme as you gather these things along the way. But you will need a basic idea of what you want to do, why you want to do it, why it is needed and an idea of how you might go about it. Very few PhDs go strictly according to plan, and your focus and direction will most likely change as your research reveals new challenges and information. But your initial motivation for doing a PhD will indicate how you will be able to adapt to challenging circumstances, your potential to master new methods and approaches as needed and your potential to produce a credible thesis at the end – in essence, your chances of success.

As recognized by the European Commission (2015, p8) and other agencies, 'There is a lack of systematic knowledge, data and indicators on study success in Europe'. While such information can be found, it is seldom in a form that equips potential students to make an informed decision about whether they should commit to doing a PhD. So, a good starting point for your PhD journey is to think about why you want to do a PhD.

Good reasons to do a PhD

Ideally you will have noticed some issue or problem that exists in a certain field, and based on your previous experience or studies, you will give the university a reason to believe that you can investigate it (either alone or as part of a research group) to find an answer or solution. You must be able to show your potential to complete the research not only in terms of academic potential, but also through personal attributes such as commitment, discipline, maturity, professionalism and self-awareness. You will also be able to show a baseline knowledge of what has been done in the field so far and how your planned work fits into it, and without this knowledge, you will likely be unable to justify a need for your research. On a personal level, you will have an idea of what doing the PhD will achieve for you in terms of your career goals and life aspirations (Table 1.1).

However, there are also some bad motivations for doing a PhD, and these are all too common and perhaps contribute to the high dropout rates seen around the world.

Bad motivations for doing a PhD

Seeing a PhD as a marker of how 'smart' you are

To complete a PhD you have to be 'smart', but the degree represents only what you have done in that instance and does not always extend to other areas of life. During your journey you will meet lots of PhD holders who are not so expert in certain areas (i.e. different disciplinary approaches, inter-personal communication, teaching skills, etc.), despite being demonstrable experts in their research field. Because

Table 1.1 Positive motivations for doing a PhD

1.	You have a cutting-edge idea for research you want to pursue, and doing a PhD will allow you to do so. You want to achieve something significant.	**Intellectual curiosity**
2.	There is an area of research that attracts you, and you feel you may be able to contribute to it.	
3.	You want to become an expert in a particular field, with an aim to pursue a related career. You want to discover or learn something new.	
4.	You enjoy the academic environment and wish to challenge yourself academically. You believe you can do it.	**Academic and career improvement**
5.	You have the opportunity to study for a PhD and want to invest in yourself.	
6.	You want to develop transferable skills that will help you in your career/life course.	

you've done quite well in your undergraduate and master's studies, you may feel that doing a PhD will just be the next step up the academic ladder. But although we often talk of 'PhD study' and 'PhD students', your PhD depends mainly on independent research and learning, so it is entirely different from a taught university programme. Indeed, you will find a PhD difficult if you expect to be 'taught' to reach a level that gets you over the finish line. So even if you have a good academic record, you will still have to have an idea or plan that others in academia can readily understand and support.

Getting a PhD because you want to be recognized or respected

Being accepted onto a PhD programme is an achievement in itself, and the award of a PhD will show that you have accomplished an incredibly difficult task. However, within academia and science, having a PhD is 'normal' and few tenured academics can be found without a doctoral-level qualification. While a PhD shows that you can complete research and other academic tasks to a high level, it is how you use your skills and research that will gain you respect when you graduate. Indeed, starting a programme and failing to complete it can potentially have an opposite effect in terms of how others see you and how you see yourself, and this can have long-lasting detrimental impacts. So, proper preparation and planning before you start your PhD will significantly reduce your chances of having to 'survive your PhD' in order to cross the finish line.

Doing a PhD because somebody else did or wishes they had

People do different things in life, and it is difficult not to draw comparisons. While it is important to 'be the best you' and have ambitions and goals, most people can perform very well in their life and career *without* having a PhD – it is not a necessary requirement for happiness or accomplishment. Again, it is what we do with our lives that determines our success, so even if we have a diploma on the wall or 'Dr.' on our credit card, this does not measure who we are or what we are worth. If your career and lifegoals would benefit from an earned research degree, this is fine (it is just one path of many), but it is equally good to simply do something different instead. The evidence produced in the next chapter shows that having a PhD will not guarantee you a good job or high income, so going through the hardships of PhD study will not necessarily pay off unless you have a clear idea of where you want to go in life, what is important to you and your realistic chances of achieving your goals.

Doing a PhD for short-term personal gain

Study can be seen as a way of getting some form of income (e.g. through scholarships or study grants). It may also be a way of putting off getting a job, stopping doing a job you don't like, or allowing you to gain or extend a visa to live in a particular country. However, your PhD study will come to an end at some point, and your financial and personal circumstances will still be there. You may have to pay back any funding you received if you do not complete your studies, and you will certainly have to manage any debt you have built up over the process.

Your ability to work may also affect your residency status if studying abroad, and you may have to return to your country of origin if you no longer meet residency requirements. Given the low rates of PhD completion that are reported worldwide, undertaking a PhD can pose a significant risk if successful completion is a necessary outcome to balance your personal and financial commitments. So, while it is good to have positive hopes and dreams, you should also consider what might happen if things do not go as planned.

2 Common misconceptions about doing a PhD
Completion, value and employment potential

Having a PhD is an increasingly popular aspiration. Only 1.1% of 25- to 64-year-olds have one (Hutt 2019), and a doctorate is the highest academic achievement you can obtain. However, in some national reports only slightly more than 50% of those who take on a PhD actually graduate (Lani 2020). These reported figures vary and differ in both availability and scope. In the US (which is the most consistently and openly reported source), completion rates from 1950 to 2000 averaged 61% (Council of Graduate Schools 2004: see Figure 2.1), but by 2012 that average had gone down to 57% (O'Shaughnessy 2012). According to the OECD, enrolment in advanced research programs in the US and Canada rose by approximately 70% from 1998 to 2012 (Litalien 2015), and a similar increase in enrolment has been noted in other countries. However, low graduation rates are not uncommon, and while some sources in Australia (ANU 2019; Hancock et al. 2019) claim that 70–80% of students complete their PhDs (but not including professional doctorates), others show that from 2010 to 2016, the national completion rate for master's/PhD programmes was as low as 14.9% (Khan 2018; Australian Government 2020a). Given the lack of clarity in the way such statistics are used (and perhaps manipulated), it is difficult to envisage a prospective student finding the information they need. Data for other regions is difficult to find in official reports, but, for example, in Kenya the (British Council-DAAD report 2018, p11) states a national PhD completion rate of only 11%.

Undergraduate degrees commonly have a completion rate of over 90%, yet UK data places doctoral completion at around 70% (Jump 2013). However, when looking at students who started their programmes in the years 2000–2001, 2001–2002 and 2002–2003, some UK universities had as few as 34% of their full-time domestic and European Union students qualify within seven years (against a Higher Education Funding Council [HEFCE] benchmark of 78%), and only

14   *The realities of doing a PhD*

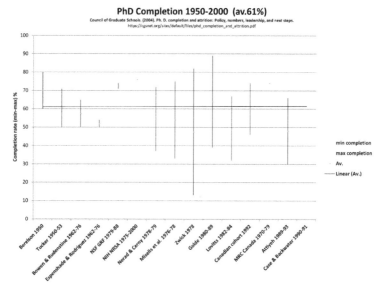

Figure 2.1 PhD completion, 1950–2000 (Author's own figure). *Source*: Data obtained from (Council of Graduate Schools data 2004): https://cgsnet.org/sites/default/files/phd_completion_and_attrition.pdf

10% (against a benchmark of 75%) of their international students (Jump 2010). But in the same data, there are also universities that exceeded the set benchmarks, with 95% of their students graduating. For the three-year period covered in the UK data, the average completion rate over the (six) best- and (five) worst-performing universities was 66.9% (Jump 2010). Therefore, the choice of university you attend is important, although current data for completion is not readily available in collated national statistics or on university webpages to help students make such decisions.

Interestingly, the European Commission (2015) study of dropout and completion in higher education in Europe covers 35 countries and presents data for bachelor's and master's programmes, yet doctoral study is notably missing from their report. However, the European University Association (2019) surveyed 311 European institutions and found that despite overall improvements in doctoral completion, 34% of candidates still fail to finish their doctoral dissertation within six years (against a recommended time of three to four years), with many of these students expected to have dropped out.

Given the lack of consistent data across countries, it would appear that while the provision of tertiary education is an important aspect of societal development, little attention has been given to the consequences of PhD dropout and completion. Relating to the UK study of 2000–2002 PhD student completion (Jump 2010), it is interesting to note that at the time, the Higher Education Funding Council strategy made no link between qualification rates and funding, so it appears that there is no direct financial incentive for universities to take decisive action for substandard completion rates. Indeed, even reports published by sector bodies are sometimes difficult to follow and apply. For example, when discussing 'research outcomes', Universities Australia (2019, p. 63) highlight the fact that over the last two decades the number of higher research degree students has doubled, with a 61% increase in domestic completion and a fourfold increase in international completion. The earlier section of the report on attrition and completion rates (p. 43) considers only undergraduate attrition, so the picture for Australian PhD students is incomplete, especially for those looking to inform a potential study decision.

Whichever of these figures you choose to use, there is a baseline truth: although PhD programmes accept provenly bright people with an accepted research plan and perceived potential to see their work through, there is a 30%–50% chance they will fail to complete their degree, and in global figures, this could involve hundreds of thousands of individuals.

For those who do complete their degrees, a PhD or doctorate does not necessarily guarantee an academic position or success in the outside world. Here are three common misconceptions that students (and others) hold about doing a PhD.

It takes 3 years to get a PhD

Most scholarships for PhD study are issued for a period of 3 years full time, but in reality, completing a PhD can take much longer. In the US, a recent study found a PhD took an average of 5.8 years (Kowarski 2019), and in the UK. a PhD lasts 3–4 years full-time and 6–7 years part-time (Higginbotham 2018). In Germany (Jaksztat et al. 2012), an average doctorate takes between 4.3 years (mathematics/natural sciences) and 5.1 years (humanities).

Striving to complete a PhD during a fixed funded period can be stressful, and extending beyond this period may require you to find paid work, leaving you less time to spend on your dissertation. There are cases in which a PhD has been done in under three years, and three years is common for STEM subjects. However, 7.1 years is more common in humanities and arts doctorates (Kowarski 2019). According to the 2014 Survey of Earned Doctorates in the US, life science PhDs took 7.7 years to complete; physical sciences, 6.5 years; social sciences, 8.7; engineering, 6.7; education, 14.2; and humanities, 10.7 years (1994–2014) (NCSES 2016). According to US Council of Graduate Schools data (Sowell 2008), only 4.6% of PhDs were completed within the 3-year period that many funded programmes offer, and the overall completion rate of 56.6% was only reached after a 10-year period. So, according to this data, you may have only a single-figure chance of completing within 3 years and a 50:50 chance if you hang in for 10 years. However, most universities will not let you continue PhD studies much beyond their published part-time maximum limit without a good reason.

To offer a comparison between PhD and master's-level research degrees, the HEFCE 2012 report (detailed by Brunt 2013) shows the qualification times from postgraduate research degrees (MPhil) for UK universities in 2008–2009 and 2009–2010 by institution. Of those who qualified from a full-time programme, only 2.2% qualified at the 3-year point; 42.3% qualified at the 5-year point, and 25.1% qualified at the 7-year point or beyond. So even a master's-level research degree takes time to complete, and it would therefore seem that the concept of funding a PhD for completion in 3 years is somewhat unrealistic.

- *Points for student consideration*:
  Students should make contingency plans to cope financially in case their PhD studies extend beyond their funded period.
- *Points for university/institution consideration*:
  Universities and funders should re-evaluate the support and funding of 3-year doctoral degrees as an achievable goal as this is generally unattainable. Promoting 3-year programmes may increase student and faculty stress as they strive to meet unrealistically challenging deadlines. Extending beyond a funded 3-year period necessitates further funding and support, and this leads to high levels of student debt (covered later in detail). To this end, promoting a 3-year PhD programme may be misrepresentative of the likely timescale (and commitment) students need to complete.

Having a PhD will be seen as a unique achievement

Despite its uniqueness in the global population, having a PhD is not uncommon. Hutt (2019) cites that the US alone produced 71,000 doctoral graduates in 2017 (although the National Science Foundation (2018) cites this figure as 54,664), and the numbers of doctoral graduates across OECD countries rose 8% between 2013 and 2017. Since

2000, the number of doctoral degree holders in the US has more than doubled to 4.5 million, and about 13.1% of US adults have a master's, professional degree or doctorate (US Census Bureau 2019).

Having a PhD is nowadays a minimum requirement for tenure-track employment in academia, so in this sector, a PhD is 'normal'. However, the quality of PhD programmes differs significantly from country to country and between institutions. While your publication record and degrees will constantly be checked in academic settings and employment, the superficial view of a PhD as a meaningful credential has lessened in its societal value, so while relatively unique per capita, its surface value is not as revered as it once was. The proliferation of degree mills (fake degrees) and cases of high-profile plagiarism and cheating increasingly coming to light in the media have also lessened the perception of a PhD, and an academic degree is not always going to be taken at face value as a marker of someone's broader worth or accomplishment. High profile cases of politicians in e.g. Germany (2006), Romania (2012), Russia (2006) and Ukraine (2017) have all revealed either fake or plagiarized doctoral degrees, obtained to boost the reputation of the holder (Harris 2019). According to Ezell and Bear (2012), thousands of unrecognized or fake universities around the world are selling fake degrees, and there is enough global demand to make this a billion-dollar business. This suggests that a PhD is seen as a desirable attribute by employers. But outside academia, a PhD may in fact signal that you are simultaneously underqualified for a job that does not align exactly with the training and skills of your degree, and overqualified in that employers may have to re-train you to fit their requirements (Arnold 2014). Thus, while professional doctorates may be more closely tied to a specific domain or employment sphere (as well as keeping people more closely tied to the workplace while studying), the value of obtaining a PhD lies almost exclusively within academia and research. But, given the 'normality' of a PhD in academia and the available data on PhD employment that is presented in the following sections, while gaining a PhD may be superficially impressive, it may not necessarily be useful (Arnold 2014).

- *Points for student consideration*:
  Students should strongly consider the nature of their doctoral degree (i.e. PhD or professional doctorate) in terms of how they will use it to further life and career goals.
- *Points for university/institution consideration*:
  Universities and funders should re-evaluate the support and funding of doctoral degrees and provide clear indicators as to how

students can use the qualification they gain. Crucially, universities should provide a comprehensive and mandatory advisory service for all PhD applicants that stretches beyond academic/study considerations.

A PhD will help you get a good job

You would think that having the ultimate academic qualification would prepare the way for a high-flying career in academia or industry, but this is not the case. The overall data on employment after completing a PhD is superficially positive and cites unemployment figures as low as 2.1% (Mervis 2016) compared to a national average of 7.5% in the US, and 3% in the UK (Vitae 2020) compared to a national average of 3.81% in 2019. However, these figures do not account for 'underemployment' (where a PhD holder does a job that does not require their PhD), and 'postdoc' employment in academia which is the biggest employment category in higher education but is low paid, temporary or sessional, classed as a training position and often non-contractual. When this is taken into account, some 60% of PhDs can expect to end up in relatively low-paid training positions, increasing to 80% in the life sciences (The Cheeky Scientist 2018). McDowell (2016) summed up the implications of sparse and misrepresented employment data in *Science* magazine:

> Making proclamations about the scientific enterprise based on sparse employment and career data about junior scientists has become a common endeavor. But this approach is fundamentally flawed. The unemployment data for Ph.D. scientists is so beset by caveats, exceptions, and holes that it is essentially useless for informing the ongoing discussion about whether the current research enterprise serves trainees as it should.

The same can be said for data on PhD completion, and given that little information of this type is made openly available to prospective PhD students, it is hardly surprising that many find themselves met with an entirely different reality from what they were expecting. Indeed, if they put faith in the positive outlook of 'thousands of successful graduates' and 'high rates of gainfully employed PhDs', one can argue that they are perhaps being misled by the academy. Even once in the system, the idea of 'working in academia' is if anything encouraged and in Australia, research students make up 57% of university research teams (Horta et al. 2018). But, given the high level of commitment in taking on a PhD, it is hardly surprising that they struggle through as best they can, and that such realizations lead them to enter the postdoc system almost as supplicants, as opposed to the qualified professionals they are.

In the UK, a report by The Royal Society (2010) found that just 3.5% of science PhDs secured permanent academic positions. Only 0.45% of PhDs continued on to become a tenured university professor (fewer than 1 in 200), while 3.5% became permanent research staff, and 53% left academia to pursue careers outside science. [*Author note*: the illustration used in the report has been criticized as being non-representative (i.e. the lines used were not proportionate to the scale of data) and the data progression in the figure was unclear (there was missing input data and terms were not defined). However, the actual data of the study stands unchallenged.]

According to the 2014 Survey of Earned Doctorates in the US, actual unemployment in life science PhDs stood at 42.1%; physical sciences, 36.2%; social sciences, 31.2%; engineering, 43%; education, 35.4%; and humanities, 45.7% (NCSES 2016). Of the PhDs surveyed, 39% of those employed in academia had taken up postdoc positions paying just over $40,000 per year. In 2018, the entry-level postdoc salary in the US was listed at $50,004, reaching $61,208 for a 7th postdoc or more (NIAID 2020). Contrastingly, the Survey of Earned Doctorates report (NCSES 2016) found that entrance-level salaries for graduates with only a BA degree was $45,478 in 2014. US data (Bauman 2020) also shows that graduate assistants do not even earn a living wage in many cities, so it is clear that investing time and money into achieving a PhD will not always bring you more money.

However, it is common to see claims such as "In 2017, on average a person with an advanced degree earned 3.7 times as much as a high school dropout" (US Census Bureau 2019) that are positively spun to show it's worth going to university, yet do not reflect the practical reality of doing a PhD. In 2018, the difference in entry-level earnings between bachelor's and doctoral degree holders was less than $5,000 (NIAID 2020). So, it has to be asked whether this margin of difference is a fair return for perhaps 10 added years of study on minimal income, any education-related debt that is built up (averaging $98,800 in the US (McFarland et al. 2018) and £50,000 in the UK (Which? 2020)), and the hardships that new PhD holders face in the job market, despite having the highest-level degree possible.

Slightly more appealing job prospects are seen in the increasing number of associate or adjunct professor positions that are being made available. But again, these are *contingent faculty* who are non-tenure track, full or part time, often set-term, and paid less (Coalition on the Academic Workforce 2012). These practices have not gone unnoticed, and the OECD (2020) has warned universities against shifting academics on to short-term or zero-hour contracts. Yet despite calls for better academic job security, scarce and low-paid postdoc employment is still growing as the realistic career path for many new PhDs.

Recent data (Woolston 2018) has shown that very few postdoctoral researchers land academic positions and also suggests that the skills postdocs learn are not necessarily sought after by employers outside academia. So, while becoming a tenured professor can seem like a reasonable goal once you have earned a PhD, your chances of doing so are in fact slim. Although landing any sort of academic position can be viewed as making progress towards making tenure as a professor, in the UK, the climate of a casualized academic labour force has been seen as dehumanizing to those following this path, and as reducing a massive body of well-qualified PhD holders to the status of 'second-class academic citizens' (University and College Union 2020). As such, the available data shows that your hopes of achieving an academic career must be considered realistically before you commit a significant amount of time, effort and financial resources into doing a PhD.

This book is being written during the 2020 COVID-19 pandemic that has rocked global economies, and employment prospects have been greatly affected. Canadian economist Brendon Bernard (2020) shows that the number of employees in lower-paying occupations was down 30% year-on-year in April 2020, and mid-wage employment was down 20%. However, the employees in high-wage occupations decreased by only 1.3% over the same time frame (see Figure 2.2).

Such conditions are to be seen the world over, so given that the academic workforce relies heavily on lower- to mid-paid employment tracks, your chances of gaining full-time employment at anything less than full professor grade are likely to be further reduced from pre-pandemic levels. The COVID-19-related crisis acts as a litmus test of where higher-education institutions in countries such as the UK, the US and Australia direct their cost-saving efforts when facing a major loss of fee income (e.g. international student enrolment). Unsurprisingly, those in the casualized and fixed-term workforce are being first to be cut, resulting in thousands of job losses (see e.g. Baker, Ross & Basken 2020). As such, the idea of an adjunct career path leading to tenured employment becomes even less likely.

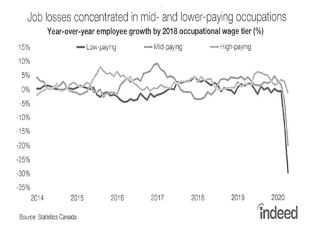

Figure 2.2 Job losses concentrated in mid- and lower-paying occupations. *Source*: Bernard (2020); graph reproduced with kind permission of Brendon Bernard. Data taken from Labour Force Survey produced by Statistics Canada (2020).

- *Points for student consideration*:
  Students should strongly consider the nature of their doctoral degree (i.e. PhD or professional doctorate) in terms of how they will use it to further life and career goals. In particular, they should consider how a standard PhD is aligned with the academic workplace, and balance this with the paucity and precariousness of academic jobs. Markedly, doing a top-level academic degree will not provide an automatic pathway to an academic career.

- *Points for university/institution consideration*:
  Universities and funders should consider how current PhD programme provision is realistically balanced with the availability of a solid career path in academia. Also, it is reasonable to question whether casualized labour and job opportunities are a reasonable return for those who have achieved the highest possible qualification universities have to offer, often sacrificing years of time and at considerable financial and personal cost. While such considerations are likely to be complex and lengthy, it should be remembered that thousands of new PhDs are being created every year, and a significant proportion of them are unable to find full-time employment commensurate and in line with their qualification.

3 Emotions and wellbeing during a PhD

A recent thread of educational research has highlighted alarming trends in adverse mental health and wellbeing among graduate and post-graduate students in universities. Consistent reports from the UK, US, Europe and Asia have shown that these students suffer severe levels of stress and anxiety at levels way above the national average.

A wide-scale study of 2,279 PhD students (90%) and master's students (10%) from 26 countries and 234 institutions looked for the presence of diagnosable moderate-to-severe anxiety and depression using clinically validated scales (Evans et al. 2018). The study found that 41% of the graduate students scored as having *moderate-to-severe anxiety* on the GAD07 scale and 39% had *moderate-to-severe depression*. This incidence is 10 times greater than that seen in the general global population (Bira et al. 2019). Furthermore, the UK reports high rates of student suicide, with 1 university student taking their own life every 4 days in 2017 (Shackle 2019), and 1 every 3.8 days in 2018 (Office for National Statistics 2018).

A US study found that more than 34% of the graduate students surveyed had *moderate-to-severe depression*, 7.3% reported suicidal thoughts, and 2.3% reported having plans for suicide (Garcia-Williams et al. 2014). A recent UK study (Cornell 2020) using data from 1,069 PhD students found that over one-third (37%) had actively sought help for anxiety or depression caused by PhD study.

A 2017 national study from Sweden (Lageborn et al. 2017) spanning 18 years found that suicide accounted for 36.4% of all student deaths which occurred during ongoing university studies. Cornell (2020) further found that 80% of PhD students believe a career in research can be lonely and isolating, 25% felt that they had been bullied and 20% felt that they had experienced some form of discrimination. So, when you consider that these percentages represent hundreds (if not thousands) of students that have been negatively affected by their PhD experience, then such reports should not be taken lightly. When completion and wellbeing statistics are applied to UK, US and European populations, these numbers become perhaps more meaningful (Table 3.1 and 3.2).

As well as study-related issues, off-campus factors such as finance, work and relationships have been highlighted as being harmful to students' mental health and wellbeing, and studying for a PhD may compound any pre-existing conditions. Especially, a PhD is unlike any other level of tertiary education and is conducted with a high degree of personal independence. While supervisors will guide you through the process, they may not be directly involved in your research. The planning, conduct and reporting of your PhD work is often carried out with the oversight guidance of your supervisor or research group,

Table 3.1 Doctoral Programmes and Wellbeing 2017

	UK	*US*	*Europe*
Doctoral students registered	**100,275** (Higher Education Statistics Agency 2019)	**Not available** A 46% dropout adjustment = 71,145 but this is unlikely to be accurate given the disparity with UK registration and graduation numbers	**764,400** (European Science Foundation 2017/ Eurostat 2019)
Doctorates awarded	**24,850** (Higher Education Statistics Agency 2019)	**54,664** (National Science Foundation 2018)	**Not available** −34% dropout adjustment = **504,504**

Table 3.2 Wellbeing and dropout related to published PhD populations

	UK	*US*	*Europe*
Predicted number of doctoral students with moderate-to-severe anxiety (41%) and depression (39%) (Evans et al. 2018)	**40,110**	*Not able to be reliably estimated*	**305,760**
Estimated number of dropouts at national rates	**31,085** (31%)	**54,664** (46%)	**259,896** (34%)

but the compilation of your PhD thesis or dissertation is entirely a solo effort, and this is what earns you your doctorate. As mentioned earlier, the term 'ABD' (all but dissertation) has arisen where people show on their CVs that they have completed their PhD coursework but have not gone on to complete their thesis or dissertation. Thus, being accepted and doing well on coursework is not enough to achieve a PhD, and according to available mainstream statistics and published research, you are highly likely to encounter stressful situations that may have a negative impact on your mental health and wellbeing.

Doing a PhD is intellectually demanding, but it also involves times when you experience isolation, question your abilities, strive to get your project through approvals and funding boards, as well as having to conduct it amid the ups and downs of daily life. You will learn and master new skills and ways of thinking (often on your own), and these will change both you and your work. As a result, the long period during which you do your PhD will probably change you as a person, which in turn will affect those around us. Most of us embrace this as a chance to develop, yet others (quite justifiably) like who they are and decide not to carry on. So, rather than being seen as 'failure', the decision to withdraw from a PhD is perhaps one of the most intelligent decisions you might make in certain circumstances; but it will always leave a mark on your life course as 'something you did not see through'. It is therefore of vital importance to recognize that pursuing a PhD is not for everyone, and not to do a PhD can also be a correct choice. As your life situation changes, there is nothing to stop you from picking it up again in the future, but if you have any doubt as to whether the years of commitment and hardship (emotional, social and financial) will pay off, then a PhD is definitely not something that you should rush into.

That said …

Doing a PhD is an immensely positive thing when things work out! Whereas other programmes of higher education are generally taught and rigid, a PhD is liberatingly open. As long as you can convince others of what you are doing and can 'walk the walk' of a researcher, you have the freedom to decide what you are going to do, how you are going to do it and how you are going to present the finished research.

When you complete successfully, you have the proud knowledge that the work you have produced was all your own doing, and you have achieved the highest-level award that universities generally have to offer. You will have made an original contribution to your field (big or small), be an acknowledged expert in your area (by way of your thesis) and have fully earned the title of 'Doctor'. As mentioned earlier, only 1.1% of the world's adult population are similarly qualified, and it is a transformative achievement in terms of personal development and potential. For many, doing a PhD is one of the ultimate tests they will put themselves through, and to come out 'on top' is a special feeling that few others experience. Even if things go to plan, you will still have emotional ups and downs, but the reward is well worth it!

- *Points for student consideration*:
  Students should strongly consider how they will handle the aspects of high-level study and the isolation of doing a PhD, on top of the impacts of other life circumstances and commitments. They should also recognize that experiencing adverse mental health and wellbeing is a probability, not a possibility. Existing conditions should be taken into account, and students should plan how to stay in regular contact with others and to discuss how things are going. Students should also familiarize themselves with university and public resources that can offer help and support when things get difficult.
- *Points for university/institution consideration*:
  Universities and funders should consider how current PhD programmes actively impact on the mental health and wellbeing of their students. They should further recognize that in the absence of existing conditions, the PhD process is causative (directly or indirectly) of the high levels of moderate-to-severe anxiety and depression reported in a range of published studies. In face of this evidence, universities should shift their management approach from post-hoc counselling provision, toward investigating and reducing causes of adverse student mental health to a minimum possible level, in line with the responsibilities they hold as workplace providers. Given the figures associated with wellbeing and dropout across the international spectrum (also extending to staff in the academic workplace), the urgency of this issue cannot be stressed too strongly.

Having looked at the general realities of PhD study from an international perspective, the next section of this book will help you assess your personal situation to do a PhD.

4 Assessing your own situation to do a PhD

Time, social commitments, finance and scholarships, international study, special needs

A PhD is a long process that demands total commitment and dedication. It requires time, costs potentially considerable sums of money, and changes your entire existence as you fit your studies and research around your daily life. These issues are seldom appreciated during the initial excitement of 'wanting to do a PhD', but their impact will be considerable not only on yourself, but also on those around you such as family, friends and colleagues. Here are some points to consider.

Part-time or full-time?

Depending on which figures you read, in the US a PhD takes an average of 5.8 (Kowarski 2019) to 9 (NCSES 2016) years. In the UK a PhD lasts 3–4 years full time and 6–7 years part-time (Higginbotham 2018). So, you will have to decide early on how long you are willing to commit to earning your PhD, and whether you are able to become a full-time student for at least 3 years, or continue with employment and do your PhD part time. Depending on your field and type of research, it may not be possible to opt for part time (e.g. if you are going to be part of a lab team or an established research group with time-limited projects), and full financial support is often made available only to full-time students. If you are intending to do your PhD part time, while your tuition fees (if there are any) may be met by your employer or the university, your daily life still goes on and will continue to make demands on your time and money.

A 2019 survey in the journal *Nature* found that 76% of the 6000+ PhD students they surveyed were spending anywhere between 41 and 80 hours per week on their PhD (Woolston 2019), and a further UK study (Cornell 2020) found the average to be 47 hours per week which is over 50% more than the average undergraduate student and three hours less than the average full-time academic. Your best-case scenario is being a full-time student managing to stay on track working 40 hours per week, but it is likely you will work more hours. Even if you do your PhD part-time and halve these hours, you are looking at anywhere between 20 and 40 hours of employed work, plus 20–30 hours of study every week. A study by Universities Australia (2018) found that four out of five domestic students had a job while studying at university.

Together with time for your routine family and social interactions, as well as time taken for yourself, you will see that a PhD intrudes heavily on your life and puts pressure on all of the social dimensions you currently manage. Furthermore, a recent 7-year study on academics working out of hours (in this case, submitting papers to journals) found that 14% of journal manuscripts were submitted over weekends and 9% during holidays (Barnett et al. 2019). So, even if you continue in academia after your PhD, your work–life balance will drastically change from what you and those closest to you are probably used to.

- *Points for student consideration*:
  Students should consider their realistic capacity to study full or part time, in conjunction with their own personal and family circumstances.
- *Points for university/institution consideration*:
  Universities and funders should ensure the matter of full- or part-time study is formally discussed with applicants prior to their commencing their PhD programme, including any considerations of work and changing circumstances.

Family and social commitments

Although you are the one doing a PhD, your decision will have an impact on your family, friends and social life. We like to imagine that the PhD will separate us somewhat from those around us, and as only 1.1% of the world's population have a PhD/doctorate (Hutt 2019), we are unlikely to be surrounded by similarly qualified people outside of a university or research setting. We may also be the first in our family to achieve such a degree, so it is easy to envisage the encouragement and support you will receive, not to mention the acclimation and acknowledgement you will get on the big day of your graduation.

But pursuing a PhD means you will be dedicating many hours of your time to research and writing. As well as 'working hours', you will be working during the evenings and on weekends. Even when not directly working on your PhD, you will be thinking about it. Ask any

PhD holder, and they will tell you that you do not switch off – you wake up at all hours of the night, you obsess over some point of an experiment, methodology or publication, and all the time, you have to keep your 'normal' life on track. Those closest to you compensate for your studies as much as they can, but every 'chore' you don't do or obligation you don't meet has to be done by someone else. Unless you cut down on time for yourself (including sleep) and the more time you spend with your 'work', the less time you have to spend with partners, children, family (especially older family) and friends. You will change, and those around you will both notice and judge you for your actions and decisions. It is easy to imagine that the situation will only last for 3 years, but as previously mentioned, this is unlikely and more likely to extend to 7 years or more (Kowarski 2019). Put this 7 years into the context of a relationship, the formative years of bring up a young family, of perhaps spending time with relatives in their later years, and it is not hard to see how tensions and difficulties arise.

But the fact is that many of those who take on a PhD actually don't graduate (see the previous statistics), so there is a 30%–50% chance that you will not make it to the end. The figures on PhD completion, employment and wellbeing are often spun to represent high numbers of people graduating and in employment, but most of these reports are imprecise, are rarely comprehensive, and do not present a clear picture of what a PhD process involves. For example, while we see that over 54,000 PhDs were awarded in the US in 2017 alone (National Science Foundation 2018), we do not see what happened to the 28,000 people who did not make it. When we read of high percentages of people being 'gainfully employed' post-PhD (Mervis 2016), this does not show what *type* of employment these people have, and whether it measures up to having earned the highest academic qualification available. Many hope a PhD will trigger an academic career ("we have a professor in the family"), but the available evidence shows that there is a very low chance that you will gain employment at a university on a full-time contract, despite having such a high-level qualification (European Science Foundation 2017). So, any thoughts that doing a PhD will improve your life in terms of money and work are not guaranteed, and even if you graduate, you may not be the 'success' that you and those around you had hoped for.

The 'F' word

People tend to avoid the word 'failure' because it is negative rather than positive, but in reality, it is something we all perceive when we don't succeed. Having enrolled on a PhD programme, if you are not awarded your PhD at the end of it, you may feel that you have failed yourself – i.e. 'I could or should have done better'. You may also feel shame and embarrassment for having 'failed' in front of supervisors whom you respect, family and friends. If you aimed to become an 'academic' but can't get a position, or if you find yourself 'underemployed' and unable to deliver the bright future or earnings you and others had hoped for, you might again feel that you have failed. However, as the evidence and statistics presented earlier show, the odds are considerably stacked against you, so 'failure' is neither unusual nor something to blame yourself for.

Many people will be involved in your PhD. All of them will want to support you, and they will make certain sacrifices along the way, ranging from just 'being there' to offering financial and family support, and investing time and effort in helping you to succeed. Their 'pay-off' is your being awarded a PhD, but their chances of collecting on their investment are not certain. From a personal perspective, doing a PhD presents a great challenge and can bring great rewards (tangible and intangible). But those closest to us will not share the same perspective and will only be able to observe your journey from the outside. There will be feelings of separation or isolation and of changed circumstances in your relationships, and while some will adapt and cope with what comes along, some relationships may not survive the course (there is no reliable data on this issue). You cannot turn back the clock to compensate for missed time with relatives and loved ones, and your social scene will move on with or without you, so the isolation of a PhD affects both you and others.

Doctoral training will involve time at university, time travelling to conferences, and vast amounts of time spent studying, researching and writing. Often your work will become 'everything', and others may suffer as a result (Figure 4.1). The fallout from these issues adds to the difficulties of doing a PhD, as well as detracting from your chances of completion. So, it is important to consider how well prepared your family is for supporting (or even co-existing) with your PhD, and how willing you are to manage and be responsible for your social commitments.

The outcome of your PhD will have an impact not only on how others see you, but also on how you see yourself, especially in comparison to others. Our perceptions of success and failure will differ, and while some will view a PhD as a great achievement, others will wonder what the big deal is. Some will see a new 'doctor' as deserving acknowledgement, while others may express disinterest or even animosity. So, however

Figure 4.1 Life-influences of a PhD.

meaningful your new title might be to you, unless it translates into a good career, increased income or some other tangible benefit, then the years of understanding, effort, support and accommodation that others have contributed to your dream may not be seen as having been so worthwhile. Taking this into account, changes in family and social relationships are to be expected, and these may have lasting consequences.

- *Points for student consideration*:
  Students should discuss the implications of doing a PhD with their families, beyond the end aspiration of gaining a doctorate. This includes matters of financial subsistence, work–life balance, time allocation and changes in routine and social relationships.
- *Points for university/institution consideration*:
  Universities should ensure that PhD applicants have given adequate consideration to the changes in routine their study will require, and that they have discussed matters with those involved. Such discussions may be undertaken in the form of pre-study counselling prior to PhD commencement, and as part of a centralized service that is separated from the role of general PhD supervision.

Financial issues

Funding your PhD is something that can impact your life severely for years to come. Even if you are one of the lucky ones to complete your doctorate, it is possible to generate huge amounts of education-related debt.

Having pursued your academic path from undergraduate to PhD, US figures show that some 12% of PhD graduates can expect to have over $70,000 (£GBP 53,000; €63,000; $AUD 101,000) of education-related student-loan debt (McKenna 2016). Further US figures (McFarland et al. 2018) show that loan balances increased for all research and professional doctorates when analysed for 2015–2016, with medical doctorates incurring $124,700–$246,000 of student debt (97% higher than 1999–2000 figures), PhDs outside the field of education $48,400–$98,800 (an increase of 104%) and non-PhD doctorates $64,500–$132,200 (an increase of 105%). Sixty per cent of master's students, 48% of doctoral students and 75% of professional doctorate students (mainly in medical/healthcare and law) held student loans. For this period, PhD graduates outside the education discipline hold an average of $98,800 (£81,675; €91,300; $AUD 153,607) in student debt (see Figure 4.2).

Figures for the UK in 2017 show an average of £50,000 ($USD 65,000; €59,000; $AUD 95,000) of student debt (Which? 2020). A national study in Australia (Universities Australia 2018) showed that 57% of the 5,874 research students surveyed felt that finances were often a "source of worry", and referring to university students in general, the study found that "One in seven domestic students say they regularly go without food or other necessities because they can't afford them".

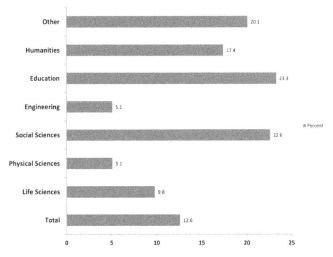

Figure 4.2 Percentage of PhD recipients with $70,000+ in Education Related Debt in 2014. *Source*: Author's own figure; US data obtained from McKenna (2016).

Many government-instituted education loans have a future earnings threshold below which you do not have to repay the loan, but if you aim to earn a decent salary after your PhD, then you are going to have to repay the money at some point. Given the relatively low percentage of PhDs that become high-level earners, any loan repayment can last well into your earning career and may influence your credit rating, your potential to, e.g., buy a house, and the amount of money you have in the future.

Scholarships

Most PhD students will be unable to self-fund their studies without either a supporting job or financing/support from their family, and they will look to obtain a scholarship for support. Ministries or Departments of Education in home or host countries are a good place to start looking for educational grants. Also, professional societies, charities and non-government organizations that have an interest in the field you wish to study can sometimes offer financial support. Employers may also offer financial support to meet study fees, or provide paid time to study.

Many countries look to encourage full-time study, and universities may offer places with a tuition fee waiver and an annual stipend. However, this will not be much – e.g. £15,000–£19,000 per year in the UK (Heidar 2019), and around $17,000–$40,000 in the US (PhD Stipends 2020), and you should be realistic about the cost of living where you intend to study. While some institutions may have additional employment for students as teaching assistants or instructors, many will either discourage or prohibit students from working alongside full-time study, or include these duties within a fellowship grant. However, a UK study (Cornell 2020) found that PhD students on the basic Research Council stipend earned less than the minimum wage.

PhD scholarships are highly sought after, and competition for them is high. In order to obtain one, you will have to demonstrate high levels of motivation and preparedness, as well as having a high potential to complete the degree. In ever-tightening economic times, nobody will give away their money lightly, and there will be many other candidates for the same award. Thus, your potential to land a paid scholarship that will support you during your studies is slim. Most scholarships are awarded for a maximum of 3 years of full-time study, so if you are dependent on the money to support you (and possibly others), you will be under immense pressure to complete the degree before your funding runs out. Given that none of the published completion figures suggest that this is likely, you will have to ensure that both you and your university have processes in place that will allow you to complete if your funded time runs out. It must be remembered that even if you do not complete your PhD, you will still be eligible to repay any student loans you have built up, and you may also be expected to pay back some or all of your grant money if you withdraw from your studies.

- *Points for student consideration*:
  Students should discuss the financial implications of doing a PhD with their families. This includes matters of financial subsistence, education-related debt and what these may mean for the future.
- *Points for university/institution consideration*:
  In recognition of a duty of care, universities should ensure that PhD applicants have given adequate consideration to any potential financial implications of undertaking PhD study. PhD applicants should also be made aware of any potential funding sources that can be approached before and during their studies, and what to do if they experience financial difficulty. Such discussions may be undertaken in the form of pre-study counselling prior to PhD commencement, and as a centralized service that is separate from the role of general PhD supervision.

International study

Studying in a different country presents both opportunities and challenges. Ultimately, you will want to study in a university that is seen as the best in your field, as it will offer you the best expertise and support. However, such places are in high demand, and these institutions are able to be highly selective as to who they admit and what lines of research they follow.

Depending on what your own country has to offer, you may consider moving abroad to study. Sometimes this may be for short-term visits, such as those funded by, e.g., European Research Area mobility programmes such as Erasmus (European Commission 2020), Fulbright (Fulbright 2020) programmes in the USA, or the ISEP programmes in Australia (Australian Government 2020a). Universities may also offer scholarships for international students from other countries to come and pursue their research; however, these are discoverable only by searching individual university websites, and they will have specific application criteria. Visa requirements may have to be met in order to visit and stay in another country. International study is widely seen as being beneficial to developing an individual student's career and international outlook, but research mobility to follow a PhD should be seen as a pursuit of excellence (i.e. the chance to do research in the best place for your study), rather than just a chance to go abroad.

There are many practical issues that may influence your chances of successful acceptance into a programme and also your overall PhD experience. Firstly, you will have to meet any entry requirements in terms of minimum grades achieved in your previous studies, approved documentation of awards and approved language proficiency (e.g. the IELTS tests that are used in the UK, US, Canada, Australia and New Zealand; IELTS 2020), as well as presenting a good application. Certain nationalities also may face passport bans or increased entry requirements when looking to enter another country, so this is something you may also need to investigate.

Culture shock

Moving to another country will have an impact on you as an individual. 'Culture shock' is a very real experience that many encounter when first living in another country. Even if the country is similar to your own (e.g. 'European', 'Asian', 'Western', etc.), there will be many differences between what you are used to, and what you will be living with day to day. Be it language and accents, food, race, appearance, religion, public conduct, hygiene or surroundings, many things will make you feel different to the host population. These differences are real, and the experience of adjusting yourself to your new surroundings is termed as 'culture shock'. The phases of culture shock are described as being the *honeymoon* (where you are open to everything being new and have a positive outlook), *negotiation* (where differences between your old and new culture create anxiety, and you may feel angry or isolated), *adjustment* (where you come to accept the new 'normal' and adopt positive attitudes towards daily life), and *adaptation* (where you are able to participate comfortably in the host culture, albeit retaining many of the traits of your original culture and self). It is important to recognize that PhD study is widely recognized as causing extreme and prolonged feelings of isolation, so moving to another country is likely to add to this problem.

Money and financial family commitments

Money is an important issue when living abroad. Few students are in a place where they can comfortably afford to live and support themselves for a long period without receiving any financial help. While a scholarship may pay for your tuition fees and offer a small personal allowance, you must see this in terms of the cost of living in your host country, and not based on what you are used to. The money you have available will affect where you live, how you travel, what you eat and how you socialize, and all of these things have an influence on how you study. Universities offer discounted meals and drinks for students, but even these may be much more expensive compared to what you are used to, so 'affordable' becomes a relative term. Depending on your visa and scholarship regulations, you may be able to work during your studies, but such work is often low paid and subject to tax deductions. This is emphasized in recent US and UK studies that found that the median wage for graduate assistants (Bauman 2020) and PhD students receiving the national stipend (Cornell 2020) was well below the recommended living wage.

When times get hard, it is easy to slip into a situation where working to keep your head above water (even if you are working within the university) can detract from the time you spend on your PhD, and this in turn threatens your chances of completing on time.

You may also have family commitments that require you to financially support or take care of loved ones. Your family may not be in a situation where they can financially support you in another country, so studying abroad may not be financially practical and needs careful consideration before you prepare any applications. Even if you are financially independent, being apart from your family and those closest to you can have emotional effects that put added strain on your studies. Although we can keep in touch via social media, Skype and the like, not 'being there' in person for family events can be difficult, and relationships can suffer. So moving to another country to study for any period of time requires discussion with all of those involved, and it cannot be seen in the same context as just financing a long trip abroad.

- *Points for student consideration*:
  Students should carefully consider the implications of doing a PhD in a different country and discuss matters seriously with their families. This includes matters of financial subsistence and maintaining ties and relationships back home.
- *Points for university/institution consideration*:
  Universities should ensure that international or 'non-local' PhD applicants are adequately prepared to study and live away from home. Supervisors and support services should also keep in regular touch with PhD students regarding how they are coping with

life away from home. Their issues will differ from undergraduate students who are generally younger, are less independent and are experiencing university for the first time. However, the isolation of PhD study can leave them overlooked and facing difficulties on their own, often without the social and support networks available to other students. This also applies to home students who have relocated at considerable distances within their own countries. Such discussions and support should be interactive and extend beyond the provision of international clubs or activities.

Special needs

Studying in higher education while managing a disability, chronic illness or learning difficulty can be challenging, and the independence of PhD study can add to the difficulties you face. However, your circumstances do not have to limit your chances of success.

Most universities are able to help in terms of accommodating any special needs you have, and have a legal obligation not to discriminate against you on the basis of any disabilities you disclose. With advance planning and discussion, they will help you to anticipate any difficulties you may face and help you to access specific support structures. You are under no obligation to inform a university of a disability or chronic illness; however, doing so will contribute towards building a trusting and supportive relationship between you and the university that will help you to achieve your goals.

The expectations for you in achieving a level of academic attainment similar to other students are non-negotiable in terms of their making an award, but universities have legal and moral obligations to make reasonable adjustments (for example, in terms of attendance requirements, examination procedures and completion time) that give you fair and reasonable chances to complete the programme. Many countries have legislation and guidelines in place that protect individuals from unfair treatment and promote a fair and more equal society (e.g. UK, Legislation.gov.uk. 2020; USA, ADA 2020; Canada, OHRC 2020; Europe, EADSNE 2006; Australia, Australian Government 2020b). Such legislation often subjects universities to a prohibition on discrimination arising from disability and imposes a duty to make reasonable adjustments. In addition, if they are aware of your situation, universities can help you to identify additional funding and support sources that can help to ease the PhD journey.

In preparing to take on a PhD, you should consider how a long PhD process will impact on your daily life, how you will interact with the university and your supervisor (directly through attendance, and indirectly through remote learning and online communication). You should also consider how you will cope with study (accessing resources, managing study time, etc.), how you will engage in external activities such as conferences or exchanges, how you will maintain your physical and mental wellbeing and where you can turn to if difficulties arise. Above all, it should be remembered that following a PhD often leads to long periods of isolation, intense thought processes, self-doubt and external critique that when un-managed can lead to depression and anxiety (Evans et al. 2018). It therefore makes sense to safeguard yourself against any circumstances that may do you potential harm, and to prepare well for any circumstances that may adversely impact on your ability to study and your overall wellbeing. Early discussion with your supervisor, university services and other students will help you identify likely problems and establish strategies for overcoming them.

- *Points for student consideration*:
  Students with a disability, chronic illness or learning difficulty should consider how they may be affected by taking on PhD study, and seek expert advice from professional and support services prior to making any application. They should also consider making their key university contacts (e.g. supervisor and study counsellor) aware of any condition that influences their ability to follow their study programme, and of any circumstances that may exacerbate the condition. Where needed, expert services and support groups can be used to help manage any changes in condition and to ensure that the student does not suffer harm or adverse influence because of an existing or emergent condition.
- *Points for university/institution consideration*:
  Universities should ensure that PhD applicants and existing students are given full opportunity to discuss any conditions openly and without fear of judgement or prejudice. When staff or faculty are made aware of conditions with which they are not familiar, they should ask direct permission from the student to consult with expert sources, including permission to disclose a student's details if appropriate. While respecting the confidential nature of such cases, university staff must also exercise a duty of care to the student and act in their best interests at all times. All staff with supervisory or

advisory duties should receive specific training in how to manage and refer students with a disability, chronic illness or learning difficulty, in a way that supports the student, preserves their dignity and autonomy, and takes fair account of their study and wellbeing circumstances.

If you've read this far and are *still* thinking about doing a PhD.. well done!

The second part of the book is about preparing your PhD application.

Part 2

Preparing your PhD application

5   Selecting your research topic and choosing a university/supervisor

Selecting your field of study/research

Your PhD should be based upon an area you are already familiar with and have some in-depth knowledge of. Above all, you will spend a minimum of three years (probably more) looking at the same thing, day in, day out, so it has to be a topic you feel passionate about and are genuinely interested in. If you lose your interest and motivation, it will be hard to complete your PhD.

Given the high levels of study and research involved in a PhD, you will be expected to have had some formal training and education in the area. As a rule, universities will look at your undergraduate and master's education records to determine your baseline academic potential, and also any professional experience that will give you further knowledge of your area. Choosing a topic that lies outside your demonstrable experience (or which is only loosely connected to it) may be interesting or attractive to you, but your potential supervisors will weigh up your expertise and experience against what they feel you will need to do to complete the research. As a PhD is a research degree as opposed to a taught program of study, this point will be examined in any application.

Do your research!

When you have identified a specific issue you wish to look at, it is important to be aware of what has been done so far in your research area, as well as to be able to explain what the current situation means for practice. This formulates your *research problem* which is your starting point. As well as your own observations, media articles, professional magazines, peer-reviewed literature and textbook sources can all be used to provide evidence or argument that a problem really exists and is ongoing, and that there is a justified need to investigate it. Considering the wide range of free online resources and communication channels available, it is fair to expect that an applicant has made reasonable efforts to conduct some preliminary research *before* applying, and this will be evident in the submitted research plan.

Your research will uncover many issues you may wish to pursue, but one will emerge above all the others to act as your principal *research focus*. Before choosing this as the topic of your PhD, you should consider how practical it will be to investigate it, and what you would need in terms of time, money, resources, etc. Some PhDs can be followed almost entirely remotely, working from home and with a minimum need for travel or specialist resources. Other topics may require specialist laboratory equipment, clinical medical or scientific facilities, placements, etc., and will be able to be pursued only at specific locations. Programmes that require unique resources and expertise will see a greater competition for places and have more rigorous application processes. So, your choice of topic may be a compromise between what research really interests you, and what you can reasonably accomplish in your personal circumstances. Not everyone can uproot their life to join a specialist research programme on the other side of the world, so it is not 'aiming low' if you select a topic that is manageable and suits your circumstances. Other people may be able to suggest a research topic for you (e.g. as part of an ongoing project), but it is important that you have enough interest in the subject yourself to keep you motivated throughout the PhD journey.

By the time you complete your PhD, you will be an expert in your field, and it is likely this will lay the foundation for your future intended career. You will also pick up many transferable skills along the way, such as a mastery of academic methods and analyses, writing reports, communicating information to varied audiences, and critically analysing situations to determine ways of improvement and development. However, without a clearly reasoned and defined topic, there will be no focus for your PhD, and it is this focal goal that keeps you going.

The thinking process for your topic selection can follow the following steps:

1. What main academic discipline (Wikipedia 2020) do you want to research in (humanities, social science, natural or formal sciences, applied science, etc.)? Do you have a background in this discipline (previous studies and/or work)?

2. What main academic sub-discipline (Wikipedia 2020) do you want to research in (e.g. Arts, History, Economics, Psychology,

Earth Science, Computer Science, Medicine and Health, etc.)? Do you have a background in this sub-discipline (previous studies and/or work)?

At this stage, you should already have something in mind that presents a 'research problem'; in other words, something that you have noticed or heard of that has not been explored in depth and presents an issue for a certain group or community. Often, the trigger for these ideas comes from personal or work experience and observations. As you explore the issue more deeply, you will refine it to a specific aspect that directs the sub-discipline or the approach you choose to investigate the problem.

3.   What branch of the sub-discipline do you want to research (e.g. African history, linguistics, constitutional law, ethics, etc.)? Do you have a demonstrable knowledge of this discipline (previous studies and/or work)?

Depending upon the nature of the issue, you will examine it from a specific angle, i.e. the ethical or legal issues of a situation, the way we communicate or think about an issue, how specific scientific processes work, etc. Your final thesis will probably combine a number of approaches and considerations that you will use to explore and answer your main research question. Even if you have no previous knowledge of an approach or method, you will be expected to educate yourself to a level where you can speak with authority when justifying your arguments and choices. Although your university will have taught programs you can take part in, most of your learning will be independent and draw on a range of learning resources. As you gather expertise, you may even add to or challenge existing knowledge and thinking in many areas.

What your research aims to do

Your research topic will aim to make a meaningful contribution to knowledge in the field. It will take the next step in a particular area, and it will produce findings or perspectives that can be used by others to inform future research and practice. Your planned research must be achievable, so while it may be desirable to solve a broad problem, your contribution will at least provide a piece of a larger puzzle. Especially if your research area is new or little explored, you may uncover issues that take priority over your original topic, and you may feel you need to change your central research topic. This is to some degree to be expected and does not necessarily mean that your original topic was 'wrong'; rather, you have uncovered issues that need to be addressed *before* your original research topic can be addressed. Research is a sequential process, and part of your developing expertise will be to direct its course to produce the most effective results. This is part of your transition from being a 'student' to becoming an independent scholar.

How to choose the right school/university

Everybody has different circumstances that direct where they want to go to study their PhD, so choosing your university is an important step. As discussed earlier, for personal or financial reasons, not everyone can relocate to study, so your choice of university will be a balance between an ideal of what you want, and where you can realistically go.

Expertise and reputation

It is tempting to select a university that has a high reputation. Some university ranking systems, such as the Times Higher Education World University Rankings (2020), look at things such as global research performance in subjects such as health, life sciences, physical sciences, psychology, business and economics, education, law, social science, computer science, engineering and technology, and arts and humanities. This produces a listing of over 1,400 institutions that can be ranked overall and by country and can highlight universities at home and abroad in terms of international reputation. Other ranking systems, such as the QS World University Rankings (2019) or the CWUR World University Rankings (2020), produce similar lists, and although they use different methodologies to produce their results, the top-tier universities (e.g. the leading universities by country or region) are similar and reflect how a university's faculty have produced highly cited research and been awarded high-level distinctions such as a Nobel Prize or Fields Medal.

Other criteria such as how a university is judged in terms of its teaching, the student options it offers, global impact, funding, internationalization and graduate employment are also featured in ranking lists, and each produces different results. But while this information can offer a general indication of how 'good' a university is, your study experience will depend mainly on how well you can make the most of what a particular university has to offer. Many top universities also offer online PhD programmes (Open Education Database 2020) which are something to consider if you have no need for specific laboratory or technical facilities and are not in a position to relocate. However, working alongside the top people in your field has the potential to open many doors in terms of knowledge development and career potential, so 'aiming high' can have many benefits beyond just 'getting a PhD'.

Finding the right supervisor or research group

Your potential supervisor will guide your research and act as your main support during your PhD journey. Not only will they be your main link to the university system and steer you through the PhD process, but they will offer advice on publishing your work, developing your research to address key and emerging issues, and developing your career. So it is important to select a supervisor who will invest both in your research project and in you as an individual. Tellingly, a UK study by Cornell (2020) found that of the 1,069 PhD students they studied, 23% would change their supervisor if they were starting their PhD anew.

Your supervisor should be active in their field and have a common interest in your research direction. They will have published widely in their field and have expressed viewpoints and perspectives that you feel are important in terms of what you intend to do. So, it is really important that you have read their published work and have viewed their online profiles on, e.g., their university web pages and external links. The research groups they lead and work with will show how they interact with others, as well as the scope of their activities. Particularly, this will indicate the scope of their international or national impact (how highly they contribute to their field), and their degree of interaction with the wider research/academic community. The Webometrics Ranking of World Universities (2020) currently lists over 28,000 institutions based on their web presence, so even the smallest accredited universities can be investigated, along with their research groups and faculty.

Once you have found a supervisor you are interested in, you should contact them directly using the contact details they provide on their institution web page. Any initial contact should be short and to the point, and professional in nature. Your contact will create their first impression of you, so you need to pay careful attention to your language, the quality of your writing and the structure of your enquiry. Write a clear subject line (e.g. 'Potential PhD research supervision in the field of _____'). Briefly introduce yourself and what you aim to do. State clearly *why* you are specifically interested in them or their group, and also a few lines on how their expertise directly links to your proposed research. Especially in Western cultures, while being polite and formal, you should avoid any overt flattery. Briefly outline how you match the admission criteria of the university (which you will have found out during your online searches), and any relevant previous education or experience you have in the area. Close with a few lines about why you feel your proposed research is important, and a polite enquiry as to whether they may be interested in supervising a PhD in the area. As an initial contact, your letter or email should give them a clear idea of what you are asking for and allow them to follow up with any requests for further details. Supervisors are very pressed for time, so the easier it is for them to get a general picture of your situation and what is needed, the more likely they are to respond. You can also attach a brief (perhaps a single page) outline of your initial proposal that they can read if they are interested, stating the research issue, the research problem and how you intend to address it. Sometimes messages are missed, so allow a few weeks for them to respond before re-sending your message. You may also include a general faculty or research group cc email contact in case the potential supervisor is away from the university or your message has been lost in their inbox or junk mail.

How potential supervisors respond to you is also a helpful indicator of how the supervisor and university work, and may inform your final decision of where to study. Getting no response or a general reference to the admissions system can be a sign that your interests may not be aligned, so you may need to carry on looking elsewhere. However, they may direct you to other people who have a closer interest in your field, and you can follow this up. Supervisory experience is often featured on faculty web pages, and those who have successfully supervised numerous doctoral dissertations can be seen as clearly able to steer you through the process. However, those with less supervisory experience, but who have demonstrable expertise and enthusiasm for your field of research, can also help guide you. So, while a 'big name' can be an attractive target to land as your supervisor, they may be in great demand, often away from the university, or their schedules may be so busy that they are not able to dedicate the time or attention you need. Because of this, many universities appoint a first and second supervisor (perhaps more), and they will divide the supervision duties between them. It is therefore worth looking at people who work alongside your first supervisor, and consider if they would be a useful addition to your supervisory process.

In cases where you are applying for an advertised PhD studentship, you are often directed straight to the application process (discussed later on). You can still approach principal investigators (PIs) or supervisors for details of the position (a contact point is often given on the advertisement), but it helps to structure your enquiries based on the main points of the advertised post, and any particular issues that they may have for you. In advertised positions there may be less flexibility with choosing your supervisor, so you basically have to take what's on offer.

Ideally, you will have a feeling that your potential supervisor is interested in your planned research, and that they are willing to offer active support and advice throughout your journey. Likewise, a potential supervisor will feel that you have identified an area of research that coincides with their own interests, and that you are capable of pursuing independent study and research to complete a PhD in the field. Your initial contact will give them clues as to how you write and communicate (which is a central part of doing a PhD), how you think about and present issues and generally, what you may be like to have as a PhD student. So, investing time and care in your initial contact is of vital importance, especially if you want to create a good first impression.

6   The PhD application process

All universities have their own application processes and will differ in some way. Some have set times (admission periods) that you can apply, while others are open.

Understanding qualifying and admission requirements

Eligibility

Depending on your country and institution, you will at least have to have a bachelor's degree with an upper second class grade (UK 2:1/US 3.2 GPA) or above. Many programmes will require a master's degree. A bachelor honours component or a master's with a research component will help show your potential to carry out your planned research. Generally, programmes that come with funding tend to set higher grade requirements, while those that self-fund may be able to apply with lower grades.

Language skills are also something you need to demonstrate, and each institution will have a list of accepted languages that may be used for study and for writing your thesis. Most universities maintain teaching in their native language, but English programmes are commonly available, and English is the preferred language of publishing academics because of its international reach. Approved documentation of language proficiency – e.g. the IELTS tests (academic) that are used in the UK, US, Canada, Australia and New Zealand – is often required for speakers of English as a second or other language, and the university will specify the required grade. Other language tests include the ETS-TOEFL (2020), Cambridge C1 Advanced/C2 Proficiency (Cambridge Assessment of English 2020a, 2020b), and the Pearson Test of English (academic; Pearson PTE (2020)).

You should view the published eligibility criteria of a programme as mandatory, and you should enquire about alternative qualifications or grades only if you have firm evidence to show why they should make an exception in your case. For published doctoral programmes that are funded by a specific sector or organization (see the section on scholarships in Chapter 4), you may also have to meet nationality criteria.

Selecting your faculty and doctoral programme

Universities tend to run doctoral education from within individual faculties, or as part of a doctoral school programme. Depending upon your topic, you will apply to the faculty or department that is most closely related to your field. This can be determined by viewing the university webpages and programme descriptions. You can also contact potential supervisors (see the earlier section on selecting the right supervisor) and discuss which doctoral programme would best fit your proposed research. Some doctoral programmes will insist that you have a supervisor lined up when you submit your application. Studying the university webpages for faculty and research groups can be a good starting point if you do not have a particular individual in mind.

Choosing the degree you wish to study for

Different doctoral degrees are awarded by different faculties. When you apply, you must specify your target degree on the application form. Again, discussions with a potential supervisor can help direct you to the right programme and ensure that you are eligible to apply for that particular degree. As previously mentioned, it is of vital importance that you select a degree type that maps with your research project and that will also support any future employment or career aims you may have.

Preparing your application documents

You need to follow the university's application instructions closely and provide all of the information required. Especially for online applications, you should study the form carefully and prepare each section in advance, assembling documents and certificates as required. Where you are required to offer, e.g., introductory or motivation statements, it is helpful to write these beforehand so you can cut/paste the required text into the application. You should follow any word count restrictions carefully, and make the most of your chance to put your case forward.

Common application details

1. *Personal data* – it is important that your details are correct and can be verified. Your contact details should be up to date, especially any email address and phone number you give as a contact point. A copy of your passport/ID card is often required.

2. *Transcripts of records /copies of certificates* – you need to supply copies of your previous education certificates and personal ID as requested. Sometimes these copies have to be certified by a professional person such as a solicitor, university administrator, etc. If the document is in a language other than those used in the target university, you may also need to supply an approved translation. Ensure that you send all of your papers as requested, as failing to do so may be seen as an incomplete application and be rejected.

3. *Curriculum vitae (CV)* – your CV should follow the format requested by the university. All of your claims and qualifications should be verifiable on request.

4. *Preliminary study plan* – if required, you should write a preliminary study plan that corresponds with the required credits and mandatory courses of the programme you are applying to. Details of available courses will be available on the institution's web pages. In cases where you are required to confirm a supervisor in advance, they will often need to agree your study plan and provide a statement of support.

5. *Preliminary research proposal* – you will need to complete a preliminary research proposal (see Chapter 7 for details of how to write this), together with a schedule for its anticipated completion. The main points of your proposal will have been discussed with your potential supervisor or university contact.

6. *Funding plan* – you will need to state how you will fund your studies. This includes any fee payments, study/research costs, scholarships, employment or self-funding. If your study visa requires that you have sufficient financial resources available, then this should also be confirmed.

7. *Supervision plan* (if required) – this may also include a statement from the supervising professor confirming your aptitude for doctoral studies.

8. *Motivation letter* (usually one page) – your motivation letter will include a brief introduction stating the programme you are applying for and why you have chosen that particular programme. You will outline your learning, teaching, research and work experience,

showing how they link to your intended PhD programme and future career development. Describe what motivates you and what you would like to achieve as a result of your studies. Towards the end of your motivation letter, you need to demonstrate the importance of your research in the context of your own life, and the bigger picture of your research field and society in general. Mainly, you need to show how the scientific/academic community and university can benefit from having *you* as a student.

9. *Any other supporting documents, e.g. letters of recommendation.*

You will submit your application online, by post, or possibly both. Each university will have an admissions office that will be able to answer any specific questions you have, but you should first study the information published on the university web pages to see if they hold the information you need. Processing PhD applications can take time, so be patient while waiting for a response. However, it is perfectly okay to ask for a confirmation of receipt if you do not hear from the university in a reasonable time, and to make further enquiries if deadlines have passed.

Warning

All of the information you supply in an application process should be truthful and verifiable by the university. In the event that it is found that you have knowingly provided false information, your studies may be terminated, any monies reclaimed and further sanctions imposed according to the laws of the host country.

---

7   Writing a research proposal

Your research proposal will help you to define your research problem, the methods you will use to carry out the research and the timeframe you will need to complete it. It also helps your potential supervisor and the admissions panel see the purpose of the study and to anticipate any problems that might arise. You present an initial research proposal (what you plan to do if accepted) as part of your doctoral programme application, and also when applying for funding or support. Applicants who will take part in an existing research project will prepare a research proposal that explains his or her part in the overall project, as they understand it. Often, this takes place in conjunction with your PI/supervisor when you have started your doctoral programme, but having a basic plan in place when you apply will help clarify your expectations of what you will be doing, and also what the PhD process will do for you.

During the research, your perspective on the research problem may change, and your proposal may need to be updated. However, your initial research proposal can be used to gauge your potential to develop the skills necessary to carry out the described plan. Even during these planning stages of a PhD, you will be required to show that you have a general education and knowledge of your chosen research field, and that you are able to isolate problems and find answers to your research questions. In particular, you will show that you can look at an issue from a new perspective, be academically critical of previous research or practices, and have a genuine desire to improve a given situation.

Each university will have its own requirements regarding the structure and content of the research proposal, including the suggested length of the plan. You should aim to cover all the required points as clearly and concisely as possible, and to give commensurate attention to each section as it is described in the application instructions.

Components of a research proposal

Background and topicality of the study

This section will introduce your topic and contextualize it to a particular situation. Be it agriculture development in a particular country, access to education for a particular group, technical developments in a particular field, etc., it will show that you have read and understood what has been done so far (both locally and internationally) and highlighted particular challenges faced by a certain group or sector. This is commonly written as a *literature review* section. The findings of your reading should then lead on to a specific area where gaps in our knowledge, abilities or technologies exist, highlighting why a particular issue emerges as problematic and why it should be addressed relative to other existing challenges. This gives a justification for proposing your *research topic* and will direct the *research questions* you put forward. Importantly, while a literature review shows that you have 'read what is out there', the outcome will show that you can see what is 'not there', why this is important, and what you feel needs to be done. This is a major starting point of both the PhD process and becoming an independent scholar.

Research topic and research questions

The title of your research topic is provisional (i.e. it will probably change by the time you write up your thesis), but it will show both the focal subject and how you aim to address it. For example: '*Increasing access to* (resource/service) *among* (specific social sector) *in* (specific area) *to address* (the identified problem): *a mixed method study* (shows how you intend to conduct the research)'. When describing your planned study, you will reiterate the research problem (i.e. the challenge or gap in knowledge/technology you have identified), and show how your research will *contribute to the scientific discussion on the topic*.

Once you have identified your concern or issue, you will decide what specific information or capability is currently missing, and how your line of research will provide some or all of the missing answers. You will then turn what you want to know and the specific concern into a *research question*. This question will not have been answered in published literature before, so you need to have done a good amount of research into your topic beforehand. You should especially bear in mind that your potential supervisors will probably have expert knowledge in the area you are investigating and will be familiar with both the published literature and the overall situation. However, this does not mean that you (as a non-PhD) cannot have come up with a new perspective or idea by yourself, so your research proposal will aim to convince them of the importance of the issue, and the need for its investigation. The more you have read and understood about your issue, the better placed you will be to ask *specific* and *answerable* questions that form the basis for your research. If little is known about an issue (i.e. if nobody has picked up on it in the research), your first sub-question may be along the lines of 'What is known about . . .?'. This supports a review-type study, and nearly all research begins with a literature review. Based on the review, you may identify new and specific areas that allow you to investigate particular issues in a certain way, so while you will retain your *over-arching research question*, you will develop new questions and approaches as you go on. However, it does no harm to anticipate what these may be like, and how they could be approached/studied. It is easier to describe how you will go about tackling a known or more concrete research issue, and you can be more definite about what you intend to do. For example, if you know that X cannot be done because of Y, but you have a reasoned theory that doing Z will solve the problem, your research becomes more experimental and easier to explain. This allows you to form a more concrete research question such as 'Will the introduction of Z in the process of Y in a particular group or context enable X to take place?' (yes-or-no answer). So your research plan will feature what you aim to do and why, together with anticipated issues, anticipated results and the anticipated contribution or benefit your work will have.

However, a PhD is not about solving a big problem, but rather about contributing to the scientific knowledge on the topic. As such, any research questions you ask should be answerable using the methods you adopt in your *research design*, and even if your research does not yield the results you had hoped for, it will have added to the scientific knowledge and moved us forward.

Research design and methods

This section will describe how you plan to conduct the research, which methods you will use, and how you justify your choices. It is advisable to read up on research methodologies, if you are not already familiar with them, and determine why a certain method is going to be the best way for you to get answers to your research question(s). Methods might include experiments, surveys, questionnaires, interviews, case studies, observations, action research, etc. You will also want to think about whether you want to obtain numbers and statistics (quantitative data); look at words, opinions, thoughts, feelings and behaviours (qualitative data); or perhaps elements of both (mixed method data). Whichever you choose, your approach should aim to get the best possible data to answer your research question.

Implications and contribution to knowledge

The 'selling point' of your proposal will be what your research will achieve for your field, and the contribution it will make to scientific knowledge. This may include improving or developing processes in a specific field or industry, informing policy, strengthening or introducing a theory or model, challenging current assumptions and behaviours, or creating a base for further research. While it is important to keep your claims grounded and realistic, projects that can 'make a difference' are going to be much better received than projects that are just 'really interesting'. Your evaluators will view the project as a whole and balance the potential 'worth' of the research against your ability to see it through. Another point worth mentioning is the connections of the study to other research and doctoral studies conducted at your chosen university and beyond. Especially, it will show an awareness of the work conducted within the university, and also any potential for outside collaboration and engagement.

References

You should back up all of your points with supporting citations in your proposal text. Full publication details should be provided in a reference list and correctly formatted as described in the application instructions or a mainstream referencing style used in your field (e.g. APA, Harvard, MLA, Vancouver, etc.). Aside from your references being 'correct' in terms of style, evaluators will look at this list as being representative of what you have read on the topic, what you have selected as being important, and also an indicator of your attention to detail (which is an important research trait).

Other requirements

In some applications, you might have to include an anticipated *research timeline* for the project, explaining what you aim to do at each stage of the PhD programme and how long it will take. You should divide this into the scheduled years of your PhD, and add in any pre-existing structures of the doctoral programme you are looking to enrol on. Things you might include are your orientation phase, mandatory study periods (courses, etc.), literature review, research design phase, data collection and analysis, publication schedules, your write-up phase, key review/milestone points, etc.

If your research requires funding and the use of materials/facilities, then you may be required to provide a potential budget proposal that outlines what you will need and why, justified costs, and any agreed or potential sources of funding. You should discuss these matters in advance with your potential PI/supervisor before your application as necessary.

Submitting your application

Before you submit your application and proposal, if you are able, wait for a day, then read it through again! It is really tempting to 'get it done', but we all often overlook small errors in language or structure, and these can create a bad impression for those reading your application. If you are new to academic writing, a useful academic language resource is the *Academic Phrasebank* produced by the University of Manchester (2020), which will provide you with "examples of some of the phraseological 'nuts and bolts' of writing". Once you have sent the application and all of the required attachments, you should receive an acknowledgement from the receiving university. It is acceptable to ask for confirmation if you do not hear anything in two weeks.

Processing applications takes time, so be patient and refer to the application guidelines and information before you make enquiries about how things are progressing. If the university has any questions or needs further information or documentation, they will contact you. However, there is no reason why you cannot continue to read around your topic in anticipation of your research going forward, and doing so helps to familiarize yourself further with the field as well as focusing your attention on particular issues that may influence your work. It should be remembered that competition for places on PhD programmes is intense, especially those that involve scholarships or places on prestigious programmes. Any rejection should not be taken personally, and universities simply choose the best available candidates to fill the available places. Reviewers/supervisors will often give reasons for any rejection, and you can use these reasons to improve future applications. Just because you may not have gotten your first choice of PhD programme, there is no reason why you cannot address any issues that come up, and apply elsewhere. If the research problem you have identified is of genuine importance to you and society, you will find a place to carry it out, even if it is only after a number of rejections. Although it is great to have done your PhD at a prestigious institution, at the end of the day, a PhD is valued regardless of which institution has granted it. So as long as your research gets done, you will have made a difference and developed yourself in the process. However, careful preparation and attention to detail will certainly improve the chances of your application being accepted, and regardless of the paths that your research and PhD experience take, the journey starts from there.

8   Planning for study life

PhDs are based mainly on independent research rather than on taught lectures and seminars, so distance learning is a possible option for many students. However, most programmes will require you to effectively engage with the university for administration processes (e.g. continued registration), supervision, taught modules, examinations and seminars. As a PhD student you are likely to spend upwards of 40 hours per week on your PhD (Woolston 2019; Cornell 2020). However, it is important that the hours you spend working on your PhD are productive and focused, and that you do not spend undue time on activities that do not progress your work (e.g. curating referencing systems you don't need, living on 'professional' social media, following interesting non-PhD projects, etc.). In order to prepare for your PhD, it is worth considering some specific things you will need to include in your application and to put together when you start your studies.

PhD study requirements

1. *Research plan* – a clear plan of what you wish to study, why, how, and what you want to achieve.
2. *Programme plan* – a written plan of how your PhD programme works, specific elements you need to achieve, timeframes, examinations/evaluations and published regulations.
3. *Access to university resources* – access to library, email and other resources, both on- and off-campus. Contact details for when things go wrong (passwords, login, etc.).
4. *Working facilities on- and off-campus* – places where you can study, access the internet, write and think – in peace! Access to hardware (computers, technical equipment, etc.), productivity software such as Microsoft Office, PDF processing programmes, analysis software

(e.g. SPSS/R), etc. is of vital importance. Additionally, you will spend long hours at your computer either conducting research, studying, or writing up your thesis. Each of us is different; however, it helps to have a reliable computer with an ability to back up data in case something goes wrong (you should do this frequently as an automatic process). Having two monitor screens makes it easier to work on one document, while, e.g., searching or doing something else on the other. Your workspace should be comfortable and have everything you need within reach. This includes making provision for you to be able to sit at the computer and look at the screen for long periods of time.

5. *Access to university learning resources* – access to courses provided by the university, together with details of any mandatory studies you must complete and the total amount of study credit you must achieve. You should determine the attendance requirements for each unit, the possibility of remote study (e.g. by internet link), and any previous evidence or learning you can use to substitute particular elements.

6. *Access to external learning resources* – you should become familiar with finding information online, trying to answer your own questions, and linking with others who can help you. Not all universities will have the courses or expertise that you need (a PhD is not a taught programme), so you need to be able to gather your information and skills from a range of sources. Linking up with online communities can be a big help in gaining access to papers, and asking your virtual colleagues questions can help with your work and thinking.

Above all, when you embark on your studies, you will need a serious commitment of self-discipline, organization, motivation and focus. When things get difficult, these attributes help to prevent you from becoming lost or swamped by your PhD, and help you to make positive and rationalized decisions, as opposed to ones that are emotionally driven.

Student life requirements

A PhD takes a long time to achieve. At best it will take 3 years of your life, and may well extend considerably beyond this. As covered in the earlier chapter, you will have made decisions as to whether to study full or part time; how you will manage your family and social commitments; how you will finance your studies and everyday life; whether to study abroad or at home; and any special needs you may have in regard to your student or personal situation, including your physical and mental wellbeing. Your situation may change throughout the PhD period, but proper planning can help keep you on course to complete your PhD and to make the best of your opportunities.

The PhD process

The PhD process differs in structure between countries and universities. Currently, there are various ways of doing a PhD or doctorate. A Professional Doctorate is geared towards professionals in sectors such as healthcare, education, engineering and manufacturing, and it includes a significant taught component with a smaller research project. These doctorates can often be completed part time and take 3–8 years to complete. A range of titles exist for these types of doctorates, including Doctor of Education (EdD), Doctor of Business Administration (DBA), Doctor of Medicine (MD) and Doctor of Engineering (EngD). *Centres for Doctoral Training* and *Doctoral Schools* within universities also offer 3–4-year programmes that combine taught modules with original research. However, a PhD is an *earned research degree* that depends on showing an *original contribution to knowledge*, presented in the form of a thesis or dissertation, and *defended against experts in the field*. Structured programmes include the Integrated or 'New Route PhD' which is a 4-year qualification involving the completion of a research master's degree in the first year, followed by a 3-year PhD programme. It may also include post-graduate courses that support learning and skill development in a particular area.

Following a successful PhD application, the applicant receives a letter to confirm their admission. Upon registration, you become an official '*PhD student*'. Depending upon your location, you may have to attend mandatory study courses and perhaps sit initial exams or deliver a successful presentation in order to progress. You may also get to develop your research proposal further at this stage, if you were not required to present one on application.

As you commence your research proper, you become a '*PhD candidate*' who is working to develop their thesis. When your thesis is almost ready for submission, PhD candidates often deliver a preliminary presentation known as a PhD confirmation, Candidacy Examination or *Lectio Praecursoria*. A successful evaluation leads you to being seen as 'confirmed' within the university, and your thesis is sent out for formal pre-examination, often to a national and international expert in your field. After a successful thesis examination and an oral viva or defence, you are awarded your PhD. In some countries (e.g. Finland), there is also a process of promotion or conferral that celebrates the formal completion and award of your doctorate, similar to the graduation events seen in most countries.

This book deliberately stops at the application stage, and there are numerous works that will help you with the stages you will encounter within the PhD process. For further information on practical and study elements of following a PhD, the following sources may be useful:

Bell, J., & Waters, S. (2014). *Doing Your Research Project: A Guide For First-Time Researchers* (6th Ed). Palgrave MacMillan.

Berry, R. (2004). *The Research Project: How to Write It* (5th Ed). Routledge Study Guides.

Cottrell, S. (2014). Dissertations and Project Reports: A Step by Step Guide. Palgrave Study Skills.

Dunleavy, P. (2003). Authoring a PhD: How to Plan, Draft, Write and Finish a Doctoral Thesis or Dissertation. Palgrave Study Skills.

Lee, A. (2020). *Successful Research Projects: A Guide for Postgraduates.* Routledge.

Murray, R. (2017). *How to Write a Thesis* (4th Ed). Open Up Study Skills.

O'Leary, Z. (2017). *The Essential Guide to Doing Your Research Project* (3rd Ed.). Sage Publishing

Trafford, V., & Leshem, S. (2008). Stepping Stones to Getting Your Doctorate. McGraw Hill and Open University Press.

Williams, K., Bethell, E., Lawton, J., Parfitt-Brown, C., Richardson, M., & Rowe, V. (2010). Planning Your PhD. Macmillan International Higher Education.

The academic development Vlog series by Tara Brabazon (2020) contains over 200 video tutorials on almost every aspect of PhD study, and it has been found to be of great help within international PhD social media groups. However, it may help you to think in advance about what sort of thesis/dissertation you are going to write.

What type of PhD thesis should you write?

After your research is complete, you will submit a thesis for examination, and it will be examined rigorously to determine if you merit the award of a doctorate. It will go to internal and external examiners who evaluate it against a set of criteria, determined by your university. If it meets the criteria you will 'pass', and if not, you will 'fail'. In the event of a 'fail', the university may grant you a chance to correct/revise your thesis for re-evaluation, or grant a master's level award that reflects your achievements within the programme.

Systems differ between universities and countries. The UK system mainly follows a grading system of 'Pass without corrections'; 'Pass with minor corrections'; 'Pass with major corrections, requires resubmission but no further oral examination'; 'Pass with major corrections, requires resubmission and a second oral examination'; 'Pass subject to doing further research, resubmission and a further oral examination'. Where a candidate fails to reach this level, a lower award of MPhil can be recommended, with 'no corrections' or 'minor corrections', an MPhil subject to major corrections and resubmission (which may also require a further oral examination), or a Fail grade.

Some systems may indicate a grade on your final certificate that represents the level you attained on your thesis evaluation, but in general, you either get it or you don't. Your performance in any study components is rarely mentioned in any PhD award, and your thesis is the main component. So, it is important to decide which type of thesis you will produce.

PhD by monograph thesis

A monograph thesis (also sometimes referred to as a dissertation) is a document submitted for an academic degree that presents the author's research and findings. The earliest PhD was developed in Germany in the 17th century, and research degrees started to appear in the UK, Europe and the US during the 19th and early 20th centuries. The monograph thesis itself has existed since doctorates were first awarded (the earliest was in France during the 12th century).

Key features

A monograph contains the entire story of your research, from beginning to end. It is often written in your national language, although the abstract or whole work may be written in English in order to make it more internationally accessible. Its length will vary, depending on the field you are working in, and STEM theses (science, technology, engineering and mathematics) tend to be shorter than, e.g., those in the humanities. At the end of the day, you will take responsibility for reporting your work in the best way you deem possible, although you will have to adhere to your university's guidelines and preferences. However, a monograph gives scope for creativity, in-depth discussion, and your overall presentation choices. As an added advantage, people may find a monograph thesis easier to prepare, as it can be done sequentially section by section and is not influenced by the external delays that come with publishing papers in peer-reviewed journals.

Main components

Title page; Abstract; Acknowledgements; Table of Contents; Introduction; Literature review; Materials/sources and methods; Themed topic chapters; Results; Discussion; Conclusions; References; Appendices.

Drawbacks

The length of a monograph may deter people from reading it, so how it is published (university press or mainstream publisher) and in which language may restrict how effectively your findings are disseminated. As such, although your work is sort of 'out there', you still often look to derive papers from your thesis in the postdoctoral stage, and academic career development often depends on your published papers and demonstrating your impact.

PhD by publication

The PhD by publication was introduced by the University of Cambridge (UK) in 1966. The idea is that you will publish your PhD research findings in peer-reviewed journals in your field, then produce a shorter-length document (a summary thesis) that brings the papers together and presents your main argument, findings and discussion. Especially in an academic climate where the pressure to publish is high, PhD by publication is becoming more popular with those thinking of pursuing an academic career or who are looking to disseminate their research more widely.

Between three and five papers will be required that have been published or accepted in mainstream journals in your field. The quality of the journal will be determined on how they are ranked in international (or national) databases such as *Journal Citation Reports* (JCR), *Web of Science* (WoS) and *Scopus*. Journals that do not feature in these databases are often seen as unsuitable (even predatory) and may not be accepted for inclusion in your PhD.

Publication types

Original research, literature reviews, case studies and methodologies. Perspectives, opinion pieces, commentaries and brief reports are unlikely to be deemed eligible for inclusion in a PhD by publication, regardless of the esteem of the journal in which they are featured.

Pros and cons

As your articles will have been peer reviewed, this is generally accepted as them having met the academic quality standards of the field. Each article can address a specific element of your research, so they can be developed as soon as you have enough reliable data to report. Once 'out there', your work is widely distributed (especially in terms of online searching) and available to your scientific/academic community. Also, the number of times that other people cite or mention your published work can also be seen as an academic quality marker. However, the publishing process is long (plan on anywhere between 6 and 18 months from submission to publication). Publishing is not easy, especially in high-ranking international journals where competition is high. Rejection and harsh critique are 'normal' (which does not make it any easier to accept), and repeated submissions, editing and re-submissions can make for a lengthy process. As such, a PhD by publication can be seen as '4 times the work' by the time you have conducted the research, written/re-written all your papers *and* written a summary or 'binding' thesis that brings them together.

PhD by prior publication/portfolio

A relatively new form of PhD exists for those who have already undertaken and produced research in their field, and can show that they have developed their research skills and subject knowledge to doctoral level *prior* to registering for the programme. This may include people entering higher education in mid-career (especially in practice-based disciplines), and the award is granted based on publications that are already in the public domain, together with a shorter introductory thesis and an oral defence. The entire process is anticipated to last about 1 year, and is seen as being equivalent to a traditional PhD student who has reached the beginning of the writing-up stage of their PhD. It should be noted that unless you have a clear track record of peer-reviewed publication and quality outputs, together with demonstrable expertise in the methodologies and practices of the field to doctoral level, you will not be eligible to apply for this type of PhD programme.

Originality and academic integrity

Before you apply to do a PhD, it is important to check your PhD regulations regarding the type of thesis/dissertation that has to be handed in at your university, and also what type is commonly preferred in your discipline. In order to have your articles and thesis included for consideration in your PhD, you must demonstrate your own significant contribution, as well as those of any co-authors. The International Committee of Medical Journal Editors (ICMJE 2020) lists the authorship criteria for published articles as:

- Substantial contributions to the conception or design of the work; or the acquisition, analysis or interpretation of data for the work;
    plus
- Drafting the work or revising it critically for important intellectual content;
    plus
- Final approval of the version to be published;
    plus
- Agreement to be accountable for all aspects of the work in ensuring that questions related to the accuracy or integrity of any part of the work are appropriately investigated and resolved.

** Supervision of a student's research project or article composition on its own does *not* constitute grounds for authorship according to these criteria. **

Academic offences

Academic offences include plagiarism, cheating, collusion, copying work, acquiring work done by others, and inappropriate re-use of your own work, among other things. Universities take academic offences very seriously, and the following matters are viewed as committing an academic offence and may result in your being sanctioned or expelled from your university:

Plagiarism (defined as the significant use of other people's work and the submission of it as though it were your own in assessed work such as dissertations, essays, articles, etc.): Your university and receiving journals will use computer software and expert analysis to detect similarity that may indicate plagiarism.

Cheating in examinations (trying to gain an unfair advantage over your fellow students).

Collusion (the deliberate attempt to gain advantage by presenting work that is not solely produced on your own or in acknowledged collaboration with others). This includes work that has been produced by another party (e.g. a 'writing service' or other individual), but may allow for language editing when the language you are presenting has been reviewed and edited by a formal service without influencing the content or meaning of your own original work. Providing material or services for other students is just as much an academic offence as using such material.

Re-using your own work (self-plagiarism). Any of your previous work must be appropriately referenced or quoted, and any re-writing or re-presentation of existing work must be significantly different from the original.

9 Being an independent learner, supervision and support

A PhD is an *earned research degree* that depends on your showing an original contribution to knowledge. In order to demonstrate this, you will have to find your own information, develop your own ways of exploring a topic that conform to your disciplinary culture, and be able to present it in a way that links with current and future practice. Often as not, as your topic will be novel (i.e. it has not been addressed in previous research), you are likely to become an (if not the) expert in this area. So, the onus is on you to gather the skills and information you need to investigate the topic, appropriate to the problems presented.

For most PhDs, the university (and its staff) are there to support your research by way of providing the necessary resources to complete your research. However, they are not there to determine what particular resources you need – that is up to you. They will help you develop, for example, your skills and knowledge in research methodologies, statistical analysis, subject principles, etc., but how you employ these in your PhD will be up to you. So, you will need to become an adept and independent researcher in order to achieve your goals. While some find this freedom to choose a liberating and empowering experience (a UK study found that 78% of the respondents really enjoyed this independence; Cornell 2020), others can feel as if they have been cut adrift by those they thought were there to help them. So, being able to be responsible for your own independent study is a crucial part of the PhD process and can make all the difference between completion or withdrawal, and how positively you experience the PhD process.

Your supervisors are there to support you as you carry out your research, and also to guide you through the university's PhD system. However, although you may develop a strong working relationship with them, they are not there to be your friend or to see that you 'pass' your PhD – that is your responsibility, and you will be given the reasonable advice, support and resources to succeed. However, the study by Cornell (2020) also found that 63% of PhD students see their supervisor for less than one hour per week, so again, independent motivation is a key quality you need to develop.

Finding your own resources and information

If the university has a visible path of expertise in your area, then it will have the necessary resources (staff, information and facilities) to assist you. University libraries stretch far beyond simply housing books and print resources. As well as giving access to journals and online publications, they can offer search facilities and expert advice on information retrieval, as well as direct you to contacts inside and outside the university who may be able to help. However, the more novel or niche your research is, the more likely it is that you will have to look beyond the university for help.

Using the web

Fortunately, in our globally connected world, it is relatively easy to contact individuals, access a range of resources and gather what we need online. People, authors and experts in your field are often contactable by their media feeds, personal websites, Twitter accounts, etc., and also through professional media platforms such as ResearchGate, Academia.edu and Mendeley. Also, mainstream social media such as Facebook offers a range of specialist groups aimed to support students and academics (see Miah 2019 for a full list of media platforms). It is important to remember that although these are 'social media' sites, you are representing yourself in a professional capacity, so interactions err towards the 'professional' and less to the 'social'. However, once you create an online presence, you will be visible to not only those closest to you, but perhaps people at your university, prospective employers and colleagues. Anything you say may be traceable or shared elsewhere, so all of your comments and actions must be carefully considered. However, caution should be taken as many of the open groups are targeted by predatory journal and ghostwriting services, so you should not reply to their posts (however attractive the offer), and you should report them to your group administrators.

Books and journal articles

Academic books are expensive, but your library should have many books (hard copy and e-books) related to your studies and general area. More specialist books can be found online, but you need not spend huge amounts of money. Most online retailers have a 'used' section where pre-owned books can be purchased cheaply and posted to you. Although it is tempting to want the latest edition (which is likely to be the most expensive), an older one may suffice for basic information and will prove useful when used in conjunction with other, more current information that you will find elsewhere.

Academic journal articles are also made available through your library, but access will depend on the type and range of subscriptions that have been purchased by the university. Open access publication is growing steadily, but authors/funders are faced with huge fees for making their work openly available. If you have difficulty accessing articles, authors and colleagues may be willing to share articles (and to some extent book chapters) for academic use, especially pre-print versions. Doctoral theses are often housed online, and there are a range of databases available (see the Open Access Theses and Dissertations (2020) website), including the Networked Digital Library of Theses and Dissertations (NDLTD 2020) and ProQuest Theses and Dissertations (PQDT 2020). Google Scholar is free and currently recognized as the most comprehensive academic search engine (Gusenbauer 2019). You can also explore university websites and contact authors directly via their online links. Other media types such as video links and podcasts are available, and many universities are offering free or low-priced online courses in different subjects.

Even if you are studying remotely or your institution has limited resources, it is possible to access a wide range of information that can help your studies. However, as with all sources of information, some are going to be more reliable than others. The quality of information relies much on the authority of the source (e.g. whether they are a recognized and accountable expert in the field), so it will be up to you to filter what they have to offer and view it in an overall context. Just because something is found online does not make it unreliable, but you should make sure you read a full range of information from different sources before taking it as 'fact'. It is also worth noting that most of the world's published research is produced in the English language, so it is important to recognize your own language skills, and any limitations this puts on you finding and understanding information. The wider and more varied your sources of information, the deeper you can explore a topic, and the richer your research and emerging thesis will be. So, language (and language resources) are important for both your research and your study life.

As a side note, it is appropriate to mention the many facilities that exist to help you organize and catalogue your references and sources. During your PhD you will save hundreds (if not thousands) of interesting articles and 'stuff' that seem really important to your work. To begin with, it is easiest to make a dedicated series of subject folders and subfolders on your computer, labelled with clear headings, into which you can save what you find. You can also make a single Word document (or its equivalent) for each main topic where you can cut/paste interesting passages and citations, as well as your own thoughts. However, it is overly tempting to start building a reference library of everything you come across, in the anticipation that it will be easy to use the formatted references in the future. In truth, as you compile your thesis, you will employ only a fraction of the work you have read, and you will often conduct new searches as you write each chapter. The same goes for producing journal articles during your PhD, so while having a highly comprehensive library of 'stuff' may seem productive, 'tech-savvy' and useful, it is easy to get sidetracked into using technology that you might not actually need. Everyone will have different needs and preferences, but it is important to focus on the process of developing your PhD *thesis*, so you need to choose carefully about how you spend your valuable time and effort.

Supervision

From the outset, your supervisor is the central link you have with the university. From your initial application, they will either have agreed to take you on as a PhD student, or been appointed to do so by the university based on their familiarity and expertise in your area of study.

The main role of a PhD supervisor is to assist and support a student throughout their academic studies. However, this is a somewhat vague statement, and most universities have a published description of the duties of the supervisor role (Table 9.1).

Table 9.1 What your supervisor *will* do

Support	Supervisors will be positive in helping you to follow and complete your PhD. They are also responsible for helping you to progress your career in terms of directing you to appropriate courses, providing opportunities to develop your skills and networks, as well as writing references and reports to support applications. They should be open to contact regarding all matters relating to your PhD and be made aware of any personal matters that may affect your wellbeing and progress.
Maintain	Supervisors will maintain regular contact with their students through personal tutorials or group meetings. They should agree a timetable for consultation, including the need for face-to-face meetings, online chat/communication and what work or progress should be reviewed. Contact should be maintained on a professional level, regardless of how well you interact. In all contact, issues must be clearly identified, together with how they will be addressed and how they will be followed up.
Advise	Supervisors will advise you as to how the PhD is done and what they would recommend in certain situations. Whether you take their advice is up to you as it is *your* PhD, not theirs. However, if you consistently fail to take their advice without discussing things and reaching an agreement, they are likely to become less supportive.
Guide	Supervisors are there to guide you through the PhD process, to inform you of the milestones you must complete in order to progress and to make sure you meet the requirements needed to allow the university to make a fair assessment. They will ensure proper records are kept with regard to student progress, and complete necessary paperwork to allow for your assessment.
Offer constructive criticism	Supervisors will receive and read written work, and will provide constructive criticism/comment in a reasonable time. They will recommend improvements and suggest corrections. It is not their responsibility to ensure you act on their observations, but failure to address any concerns may influence any recommendation they make as to whether you progress or submit your thesis. When they feel your progress is inadequate or when standards of work consistently fall below those generally expected, supervisors will report such occurrences to the Postgraduate Tutor and/or the Director of Postgraduate Studies.
Publication	Supervisors will encourage their students to publish the results of their research as they emerge and which are suitable for publication. This may be either singly as sole authors, or jointly with them as a co-author. However the duties of supervision alone are not valid criteria for asserting authorship, without conforming to the recognized and written guidelines of the respective institution *and* the target publisher.

Rule #1 of a PhD:

It is *your* PhD – not anyone else's!

Rule #2 of a PhD:

Your supervisor is not there to ensure you *pass* your PhD, but to ensure you have fair and appropriate means to do so.

The process of research degree supervision is explicated within codes of practice and learning and teaching awards, and often associated with research excellence frameworks. However, while many institutions claim to provide 'excellence in supervision', this cannot be taken at face value. A cross-country analysis of regulatory and professional frameworks in Australia, New Zealand, South Africa and the United Kingdom found that while potential competence was able to be demonstrated, there was no way of guaranteeing the excellence of a single member of staff in a complex process like the completion of a doctoral thesis, and this was not meaningfully measured in any of the main national/institutional approaches (McCulloch et al. 2016) (Table 9.2).

Notably, a UK study by Cornell (2020) found that 63% of PhD students see their supervisor for less than one hour per week, and that 23% would change their supervisor if they were starting their PhD again. So, as previously mentioned, your choice or allocation of supervisor is a crucial aspect of your PhD study.

What to do when conflicts arise

The student-supervisor relationship involves strict responsibilities for both parties. Universities often have published guidelines for both parties, and you should establish what you both expect from the student-supervisor relationship relative to these guidelines. However things do not always go smoothly, and the student-supervisor relationship is commonly cited as being a problematic area. The article published by Evans et al. (2018) concerning evidence of a mental health crisis in

Table 9.2 What your supervisor *won't* do.

Tutor	Your supervisor is not there to teach you *how* to do things, but they will advise and direct you to those who can.
Provide friendship	Your supervisor will be supportive throughout your PhD. However, this is primarily a working relationship, regardless of how well you interact or get on. They will be your main critic and have an obligation to give their honest opinion as to how you are progressing and what they think of your work. For this reason, some supervisors may appear to distance themselves from you as an individual, but their conduct should always be professional and positive.
Correct language	Supervisors (and lecturers on courses) will point out language issues (either native or non-native), but they will not usually correct or edit mistakes or errors. They will direct you to language services or courses on academic writing, but any corrections must be made by the PhD candidate themselves. A student/candidate may be able to use professional language editing services, as long as the assistance they receive does not influence or substantially alter the original work. It must be clear that the candidate/student has not attempted to pass off the writing of others as their own, and to do so may be considered an academic offence and result in sanctions, failure or discontinuation.

graduate education sparked considerable interest and concern across the globe. But while they indicated that a supportive supervisor is important for student wellbeing, their raw data indicates the main causes of adverse mental health (51%) lie directly within the student-supervisor relationship. It is therefore sensible to be aware of what you can do if difficulties arise.

Having a supervisor who doesn't seem to be engaging with you is difficult, but focusing on the problem you are trying to solve rather than your emotions will help solve many conflicts. Firstly, while critique may be difficult to hear, this is what they are paid to do, so try to look past any personal differences and listen to what they have to say. They may be hostile or seem aggressive, complain about the way you work or what you produce, always seem negative or perhaps be a know-it-all. But in amongst the feelings they provoke in you, there is normally something you can latch onto to improve your work. So, if you can recognize and act on this without coming into conflict, it will act in your best interests. As a first step, try to have reasonable and clear conversations with them, and raise any issues in an assertive but non-confrontational manner. If you mention how their critique or actions make you feel (recognizing that this is something that is in both your interests to deal with), then it is possible that you can improve the way you communicate with each other without making it a problem issue. Especially, it helps to revisit your supervision agreement or plan, and highlight areas where you can improve on the current situation. However, it is your PhD, not theirs, so you should ensure that the supervision process is positive towards achieving your goal – to get your PhD.

On the other end of the scale, some supervisors are silent or unresponsive to your requests for help or advice. This may be because they are super-busy within the university and outside, and so they are unable to give you the time you want or need. All supervision agreements should stipulate when, where and how often you will meet up, the focus of the meetings, and what each of you should have done in advance. Whether it is making a progress report, submitting a draft chapter, or simply catching up, you should be clear about what will be discussed and any actions that need to be taken. Where possible, you should have a written record (e.g. an email chain) that shows who has done what, and this can be used to structure your next steps. After physical meetings, it helps to send a quick email afterwards thanking the supervisor for their time and reiterating what you have discussed and any agreements you have made. Sometimes something will be overlooked or cause a delay in response, but this should not be a regular occurrence, and both parties should be patient with each other, albeit ensuring that the PhD process moves forward in an acceptably timely manner. If this becomes problematic, then you need to take positive steps to keep your PhD on track, taking responsibility for finding your own information and sources of support for yourself. However, if the situation is preventing you from moving forward, then you should consider taking on either a new or second supervisor who will be able to meet your needs.

Many supervisors are great and will work hard to build a productive and supporting relationship. But however positive and friendly they are, your PhD needs critical challenge to make sure it will stand up to examination (for example, by peer-reviewers in the case of a PhD by publication, or the examination board of the university who will assess your thesis). Being 'super-agreeable' is not always in your best interests, so you need to ask specific questions that require your supervisor to assess different aspects of your work, practice and performance. If they are indecisive in stating procedural points (e.g. submission procedures or processes), then you should agree upon timeframes when they will get back to you with the information, and follow things up if needed. If they are unable to answer your questions in a timely manner, you should ask them to refer you to other sources who can advise you. You can also speak with other students to get a picture of what they are doing, the information and help they receive, and how you compare. Some professors may be dominatingly assertive in how you go about your PhD ('micro-managing'), and this may be because they are genuine experts in their field and know exactly what is required to get through the PhD process. But there are others who may appear to have all the answers but in fact are just full of hot air. If you are not sure about any particular recommendations or assertions, you should firstly find out what others are doing, and attempt to find the information for yourself. You can then rekindle the discussion with your supervisor in a way that introduces the new information without challenging or embarrassing them, and moves the situation forward in a positive way.

By the time you are ready to submit, you should have no grounds to doubt that your supervisor has reviewed the content of your thesis in detail, and that there are no areas that could be anticipated as being grounds for failing your PhD. If you are in any doubt, it may be sensible to suggest that the opinion of a second supervisor or advisor may be useful to see if there are any specific areas that could be improved on before submission. This is particularly useful if your supervisor does not have expertise in your particular area of research. Although your supervisor will not be able to give you any guarantee that you will pass the final thesis examination or viva (oral defence), they should have every reasonable confidence that your thesis has covered the area with sufficient depth and detail not to fail. As your main supervisor, they should withhold any permission to submit your thesis for examination until you are at this stage. Specific feedback and discussion will help allow this to happen.

Changing your supervisor

If you reach the point where you cannot reasonably continue with your supervisor, or you feel you are in an unfair situation, then you need to take firm action to change the situation. Having taken reasonable and documented steps to discuss the situation, you may feel that a change of supervisor is appropriate. Ideally, this will be a mutual decision when both parties agree that your needs and expectations are not being met, and it is not productive to continue the current supervision relationship. However, when you can clearly demonstrate that you have performed to the required standard both in your studies and practically as a semi-independent researcher, the university should take steps to provide you with alternative or added supervision that will allow you to undergo a fair examination process. Most universities have a set process for this, and if the decision is amicable, then your current supervisor can advise you or take the process forward. Other sources of support are your postgraduate study services or doctoral school. You should be able to be accompanied to any meetings by a person who will support you through the process.

In all cases, you should present your case in a way that is unemotional and refers to the reasonable expectations laid out in your supervision agreement or policy. At all stages, you should refer to both your actions and those of your supervisor. Where a conflict has arisen or a situation has made you feel that despite reasonable efforts you have been treated unfairly, you should document what has taken place, and any evidence you may have to support your case. This is especially important where you feel your supervisor has acted either personally inappropriately, or they have abused their position of trust. Again, you should base your request to change supervisors on the existing policies of the university, and any reasonable expectations you may have as a student and as an individual. As a PhD student, you are considered part of the academic community, and you have a right to be treated with fairness and dignity.

Your main aim is to have the opportunity for a fair examination of your PhD, and not to seek any judgement for personal differences or ways of working. So while considering a change of supervisors may leave you feeling pressured by issues of hierarchy and power in the academic environment, it can be a proactive step in following your PhD path. In certain circumstances, it may be that your university is unable to resolve issues to your satisfaction. For example, if your current supervisor is unable to continue their duties due to illness or unforeseen changes in workload, or because they are leaving the university, the university will make arrangements for alternative supervision, or perhaps help you transfer your studies to another area or institution.

Where circumstances have been shown to breach university regulations or the national law, appropriate action will be taken. This may involve formal investigations being carried out, but you are not expected to tolerate or be subjected to unlawful or unethical behaviour on the part of an individual or their institution. You can also seek further advice (that should remain confidential and anonymous) outside the university if needed, and your student union can help advise you further.

Ending on a positive note!

Earning a PhD or any other form of doctorate is the crowning achievement of your education journey. It shows you have had the ambition and perseverance to see through a long period of study, conduct your own independent research and defend your position in the face of expert peer examination. Your work will have made a meaningful contribution to your field, and is something that you and others may build on in the future. Even if it is not groundbreaking in itself, others may use your ideas and methods to improve practices in their own field, and this may lead to interventions that improve, for example, education, climate change or technology advancement, or even save lives. So completing your PhD will have made a difference, and you should be proud of what you have achieved.

When you get your PhD, you will know what *you* have done, but not what other people will do with your work in the future. So this in itself is a great motivation to take the next step and apply for a PhD position. With careful and honest preparation, you stand a good chance of completing your award and setting the base for a good future career. As a result of being awarded your PhD, you will be recognized as an independent scholar and having expertise in your field. But gaining the credential is only part of the PhD process, and it is what you do with it that gives it real meaning and benefit.

What to do now?

Having read this book carefully, you will have all of the main points from which to develop a solid PhD application. As long as your proposal aligns with the aims of your target university and the research interests of potential supervisors, with supporting qualifications and motivations you will have a fair chance of competing for a coveted PhD study place. How you approach your PhD and studies has been covered in various books and differs between institutions and individual supervisors. However, by formulating a solid application and gathering the necessary evidence and information that supports it, you are already adopting the practices of an organized and focused independent researcher. The following PhD checklist will help you assess your own potential to take on a PhD and help you build a convincing PhD application.

Your PhD checklist

Questions		Ready? ✗ / ✔
1.	Why do you want to do a PhD?	Can you answer this question clearly in three minutes, describing your motivation to gain the award, your motivation to pursue your particular field of research and what you feel it will do for you and others?	
2.	Do you have a realistic idea of where your PhD may lead you?	What field of work or career path may your PhD lead to? What skills might you pick up that will help your job prospects? What skills and knowledge are needed in your employment sector? Do you need a PhD to progress?	
3.	Do you have some demonstrable knowledge and education in your chosen area?	Can you show how your previous knowledge and experience will contribute to your planned PhD? Do you have evidence of your achievements? Do you have alternative evidence of how your work or life experience can contribute to your studies?	

4.	Have you read widely (books, articles, web sources) on your subject and identified a particular issue you want to research?	Can you show that you have the ability to gather information for yourself? Can you show that you have considered varying perspectives on a particular issue, and have a justified reason for selecting your topic? Can you explain why this particular issue is important, and what it means for your field, for practice, and for the societal contribution it might make?
5.	Do you meet the eligibility criteria for your target university?	Have you read the admission criteria for your intended faculty/ programme? Can you prove (with documentation) that you meet these criteria? Can you explain why this particular university is a good fit for your intended research?
6.	Do you have a supervisor in mind?	Is there a particular member of the university you would like to supervise your PhD? Can you explain what experience or expertise they would bring, and why they should do so? Have you spoken with them about your proposed research area, and would they be willing to take you on? Are they likely to have reasonable time for you in their schedule?
7.	Do you have an idea of what subjects you will study during your PhD, and how?	Have you looked at your target university's published programmes and courses? Have you spoken with other students or advisors? Have you got study resources that you can access on- and offsite? Do you have an idea of how long your PhD might take (full or part time)?

8. Have you realistically planned how your PhD study will fit into your everyday life?	How will you manage your family and social commitments? How will you finance your studies and everyday life? Have you anticipated the issues of studying abroad or away from home? Do you have any special needs in regard to your student or personal situation, including your physical and mental wellbeing, and how will you address these needs? Are your family or close ones fully prepared for what you will do, and are they supportive?
9. Are you familiar with the application process?	Have you carefully read the application process for your particular university/programme? Have you prepared statements for each section, and gathered evidence to support your application? Do you know the process used to assess applications and when you can expect a decision?

PhD positions are highly competitive. For published positions, you will be up against other applicants who may have similar or better experience and qualifications, so the way you present yourself on paper and at interview (if applicable) is of vital importance. Not only should you ask and answer specific questions concisely, you should be able to support all of your claims with either evidence of achievement, or examples of solid experience. In essence, you need to '*be the best you*'.

Your application will likely involve an assessment of how well you have done in previous studies (e.g. your undergraduate/graduate grade or GPA), how well you do in admissions tests (e.g. the Graduate Record Examinations (GRE) that are common in the US and Canada), any previous research you have done or been involved with, letters of support or recommendation, how well you perform at interview, the relevance of your work record, your expressed goals, etc., as well as the information you supply on your application. You should anticipate any questions about your resume/CV, as well as those that will ask about your 'fit' into a particular programme. Especially, reading up on both the institution and the field you are studying will help you expand beyond the '*I'm really enthusiastic*' or '*I'm a hard worker*' type of responses, and show that you have really considered what you will gain from attending that particular university, and what you will give in return. The clearer picture you paint of what you want to achieve and how you aim to do it, the better a university can judge your potential for completion.

So, being properly prepared increases not only your chances of being accepted on to a PhD programme (the rate of which can vary anywhere between 8% and 30%), but also your chances of being awarded your PhD at the end of the journey (which is about 50% to 70% of those who start).

Considering the points raised in this book will significantly improve your chances of PhD success, but more importantly, it will help you decide whether you should actually take on a PhD in the first place. Deciding *not* to do a PhD is just as important, especially if you are likely to commit large amounts of time, effort, money and emotion into doing something that either you don't need or just isn't for you. In fact, there are very few jobs where having a PhD or professional doctorate is a mandatory requirement, and you can achieve success in many other ways. The best PhD students are happy and immersed in their work, and driven by what they might achieve or discover. But chaining yourself to something you don't like for anywhere between 3 and 10 years is not a recipe for happiness. Although being known as 'doctor' or 'professor' is enticing, the effort and hardships of PhD study (and beyond) are well documented. Hopefully, the hard questions raised in this book will help give you a real perspective of what a PhD entails, and help you make an informed decision as to whether it is really for you.

References and resources

ADA (Americans with Disabilities Act) National Network. (2020). *What is the Americans with Disabilities Act (ADA)?* Available from: https://adata.org/learn-about-ada

American Psychological Association. (2016). *Datapoint: what are the acceptance rates for graduate psychology programs?* Available from: https://www.apa.org/monitor/2016/02/datapoint

ANU [Australian National University]. (2019). *Higher degree research: trends within the contemporary Australian context.* Available from: http://w3.unisa.edu.au/staffdev/word/mandy_thomas_ppt_29june.pdf

Arnold, C. (October 2014). Overqualified or underqualified? *Science*. Available from: https://www.sciencemag.org/careers/2014/10/overqualified-or-underqualified

Australian Government – Department of Education and Training. (2020). *Enrolment statistics [Database].* Available from: http://highereducation-statistics.education.gov.au/

Australian Government – Department of Education, Skills and Employment. (2020a). *Student mobility programs.* Available from: https://internationaleducation.gov.au/International-network/Australia/policyupdates/Pages/Article-Student-Mobility-Programs.aspx

Australian Government – Department of Education, Skills and Employment. (2020b). *Higher education disability support program.* Available from: https://www.education.gov.au/higher-education-disability-support-programme

Baker, S., Ross, J., & Basken, P. (May 2020). Pandemic throws spotlight on HE employment practices. *Times Higher Education.* https://www.timeshigher-education.com/news/pandemic-throws-spotlight-he-employment-practices

Barnett, A., Mewburn, I., & Schroter, S. (2019). Working 9 to 5, not the way to make an academic living: observational analysis of manuscript and peer review submissions over time. *BMJ*, 367: l6460. Available from: https://www.bmj.com/content/367/bmj.l6460

Bauman, D. (March 2020). Do graduate assistants earn a living wage? Not in these cities. *Chronicle of Higher Education.* Available from: https://www.chronicle.com/article/Do-Graduate-Assistants-Earn-a/248169?key=sDFk4Qum8UZIcp0FmqC6TuwqKFnwBEIVNw_e50WNmw0ri6GLzf3igaAr7OGxbOBnZnlWQjB3MkNERXFXRzNuQ1lzcUY0dFI5YkN2UkhzTXpxNWN2VlBRdnVhUQ

Bernard, B. (2020). *Job losses concentrated in mid- and lower-paying occupations*. Available from: https://twitter.com/BrendonBernard_/status/1258820988181020672

Bira, L., Evans, T. M., & Vanderford, N. L. (2019). Mental health in academia: an invisible crisis. *Physiology News*, 115, 32–35. Available from: https://www.physoc.org/magazine-articles/mental-health-in-academia-an-invisible-crisis/

Brabazon, T. (2020). *Academic Development Vlog series*. Available at: https://www.youtube.com/user/TaraBrabazon

British Council. (2018). *Research and PhD capacities in Sub-Saharan Africa: Kenya report*. Available at: https://www.britishcouncil.org/sites/default/files/h233_05_research_and_phd_capacities_in_sub-saharan_africa_kenya_report_final_web.pdf

Brunt, A. (2013). Rates of qualification from postgraduate research degrees. *Higher Education Statistics Agency*. Available at: https://www.hesa.ac.uk/files/pisg/PITG_2013_02/PITG_13_08.pdf

Cambridge Assessment of English. (2020a). *C1 advanced*. Available from: https://www.cambridgeenglish.org/exams-and-tests/advanced/

Cambridge Assessment of English. (2020b). *C2 proficiency*. Available from: https://www.cambridgeenglish.org/exams-and-tests/proficiency/

Coalition on the Academic Workforce. (2012). *A portrait of part-time faculty members*. Available from: http://www.academicworkforce.org/CAW_portrait_2012.pdf

Cornell, B. (2020). *PhD life: the UK student experience*. HEPI Report 131. Higher Education Policy Council. https://www.hepi.ac.uk/wp-content/uploads/2020/06/PhD-Life_The-UK-Student-Experience_HEPI-Report-131.pdf

Council of Graduate Schools. (2004). *PhD. completion and attrition: policy, numbers, leadership, and next steps*. Available from: https://cgsnet.org/sites/default/files/phd_completion_and_attrition.pdf

CWUR. (2020). *CWUR – World University Rankings 2019–2020*. Available from: https://cwur.org/2019-2020.php

Ehrenberg, R. G., & Kuh, C. V. (Eds.). (2011). *Doctoral education and the faculty of the future*. Ithaca: Cornell University Press.

ETS-TOEFL. (2020). *The TOEFL® Test*. Available from: https://www.ets.org/toefl

European Agency for Development in Special Needs Education (EADSNE). (2006). *Special needs education in Europe (Vol. 2): provision in post-primary education*. Available from: https://www.european-agency.org/sites/default/files/special-needs-education-in-europe-volume-2-provision-in-post-primary-education_Thematic-EN.pdf

European Commission. (2015). *Dropout and completion in higher education in Europe*. Luxembourg: European Commission. Available at: https://supporthere.org/sites/default/files/dropout-completion-he_en.pdf

European Commission. (2020). *Erasmus+ programme guide*. Available from: https://ec.europa.eu/programmes/erasmus-plus/programme-guide/part-b/three-key-actions/key-action-1/mobility-higher-education-students-staff_en

European Science Foundation. (2017). *2017 Career Tracking Survey of Doctorate Holders* [Project Report]. Available from: http://www.esf.org/fileadmin/user_upload/esf/F-FINAL-Career_Tracking_Survey_2017__ Project_Report.pdf

European University Association. (2019). *Doctoral education in Europe today: approaches and institutional structures.* Available from: https://www.eua.eu/downloads/publications/online eua cde survey 16.01.2019.pdf

Eurostat. (2019). *Tertiary education statistics.* Available from: https://ec.europa.eu/eurostat/statistics-explained/index.php/Tertiary_education_statistics#Participation_by_level

Evans, T. M., Bira, L., Gastelum, J. B., Weiss, L. T., & Vanderford, N. L. (2018). Evidence for a mental health crisis in graduate education. *Nature Biotechnology*, 36(3), 282–284. Available from: https://www.nature.com/articles/nbt.4089

Ezell, A., & Bear, J. (2012). *Degree mills: the billion-dollar industry that has sold over a million fake diplomas.* Amherst: Prometheus Books.

Fulbright. (2020). *Overview.* Available from: https://us.fulbrightonline.org/about

Garcia-Williams, A. G., Moffitt, L., & Kaslow, N. J. (2014). Mental health and suicidal behavior among graduate students. *Academic Psychiatry*, 38(5), 554–560. Available from: https://link.springer.com/article/10.1007%2Fs40596-014-0041-y

Gusenbauer, M. (2019). Google Scholar to overshadow them all? Comparing the sizes of 12 academic search engines and bibliographic databases. *Scientometrics*, 118(1), 177–214. Available from: https://link.springer.com/article/10.1007%2Fs11192-018-2958-5

Hancock, S., Wakeling, P., & Chubb, J. (2019). *21st Century PhDs: Why we need better methods of tracking doctoral access, experiences and outcomes [Working Paper No.2].* Research on Research Institute. Report. https://doi.org/10.6084/m9.figshare.9917813.v1

Harris, S. (August 2019). Putin's plagiarism, fake Ukrainian degrees and other tales of world leaders accused of academic fraud. *The Conversation.* Availablefrom:https://theconversation.com/putins-plagiarism-fake-ukrainian-degrees-and-other-tales-of-world-leaders-accused-of-academic-fraud-112826

Heidar, H. (2019). *PhD funding around the world.* QS Top Universities. Available from: https://www.topuniversities.com/blog/phd-funding-around-world

Higginbotham, D. (2018). What is a PhD? *Prospects.* Available from: https://www.prospects.ac.uk/postgraduate-study/phd-study/what-is-a-phd

Higher Education Statistics Agency. (2019). Higher education student statistics: UK, 2017/18 - student numbers and characteristics. Available from: https://www.hesa.ac.uk/news/17-01-2019/sb252-higher-education-student-statistics/numbers; https://www.youtube.com/watch?v=Ftma2Nd3zkQ

Horta, H., Cattaneo, M., & Meoli, M. (2018). PhD funding as a determinant of PhD and career research performance. *Studies in Higher Education*, 43(3), 542-570. DOI: 10.1080/03075079.2016.1185406

Hutt, R. (2019). *Which countries have the most doctoral graduates?* World Eco
nomic Forum. Available from: https://www.weforum.org/agenda/2019/10/doctoral-
graduates-phd-tertiary-education/

ICMJE [International Committee of Medical Journal Editors]. (2020).
Defining the role of authors and contributors. Available from: http://www.
icmje.org/recommendations/browse/roles-and-responsibilities/defining-the-
role-of-authors-and-contributors.html

International English Language Testing System (IELTS). (2020). *About us.*
Available from: https://www.ielts.org/info-pages/about-us

Jaksztat, S., Preßler, N., Briedis, K. (2012). *Promotionen im Fokus: promotions
und Arbeitsbedingungen Promovierender im Vergleich* [Doctoral degrees in
focus: doctoral degrees and working conditions in comparison of doctoral
students]. HIS Hochschul-Informations-System GmbH. Available from:
https://www.dzhw.eu/pdf/pub_fh/fh-201215.pdf

Jump, P. (July 2010). The slow road: where PhD success comes late, if at all.
Times Higher Education. Available from: https://www.timeshighereduca-
tion.com/news/phd-completion-rates-2013/2006040.article

Jump, P. (July 2013). PhD completion rates, 2013. *Times Higher Education.*
Available from: https://www.timeshighereducation.com/news/the-slow-
road-where-phd-success-comes-late-if-at-all/412628.article

Khan, S. (July 2018). PhD completion: an evidence-based guide for students,
supervisors and universities. *The Conversation.* Available from: https://the-
conversation.com/phd-completion-an-evidence-based-guide-for-students-supervisors-
and-universities-99650

Kowarski, I. (August 2019). How long does it take to get a PhD. degree? *US
News & World Report.* Available From: https://www.usnews.com/education/
best-graduate-schools/articles/2019-08-12/how-long-does-it-take-to-get-a-phd-
degree-and-should-you-get-one

Lageborn, C. T., Ljung, R., Vaez, M., & Dahlin, M. (2017). Ongoing university
studies and the risk of suicide: a register-based nationwide cohort study of 5
million young and middle-aged individuals in Sweden, 1993–2011. *BMJ
Open*, 7(3), e014264. Available from: https://www.ncbi.nlm.nih.gov/pmc/arti-
cles/PMC5387952/

Lani, J. (2020). *Almost 50% of all doctoral students don't graduate.* Statistics
Solutions.Availablefrom:https://www.statisticssolutions.com/almost-50-of-all-doctoral-
students-dont-graduate/

Legislation.gov.uk. (2020). *Equality Act 2010.* Available from: http://www.leg-
islation.gov.uk/ukpga/2010/15/contents

Litalien, D. (2015). Improving PhD completion rates: where should we start?
The Wiley Network. Available from: https://www.wiley.com/network/
researchers/writing-and-conducting-research/improving-phd-completion-rates-where-
should-we-start

McCulloch, A., Kumar, V., van Schalkwyk, S., & Wisker, G. (2016). Excellence
in doctoral supervision: an examination of authoritative sources across four
countries in search of performance higher than competence. *Quality in
Higher Education*, 22(1), 64–77. DOI: 10.1080/13538322.2016.1144904

McDowell, G. (June 2016). The fool's gold of PhD. employment data. *Science.* Available from:https://www.sciencemag.org/careers/2016/06/fool-s-gold-phd-employment-data

McFarland, J., Hussar, B., Wang, X., Zhang, J., Wang, K., Rathbun, A., ... & Mann, F. B. (2018). *The condition of education 2018. NCES 2018-144.* National Center for Education Statistics. U.S. Department of Education. Available from: https://nces.ed.gov/programs/coe/pdf/coe_tub.pdf

McKenna, L. (April 2016). The ever-tightening job market for PhD.s: why do so many people continue to pursue doctorates? *The Atlantic.* Available from: https://www.theatlantic.com/education/archive/2016/04/bad-job-market-phds/479205/

Mervis, J. (May 2016). 'Employment crisis' for new PhD.s is an illusion. *Science.* Available from: https://www.sciencemag.org/careers/2016/05/employment-crisis-new-phds-illusion

Miah, A. (October 2019). The A to Z of social media for academia. *Times Higher Education.* Available at: https://www.timeshighereducation.com/a-z-social-media

National Center for Science and Engineering Statistics [NCSES]: Directorate for Social, Behavioral and Economic Sciences. (2016). *Doctorate recipients from U.S. universities.* Available from: http://www.nsf.gov/statistics/2016/nsf16300/digest/nsf16300.pdf

National Institute of Allergy and Infectious Diseases [NIAID]. (2020). *Salary cap and stipends.* Available from: https://www.niaid.nih.gov/grants-contracts/salary-cap-stipends

National Science Foundation. (2018). Number of doctorates awarded by US institutions in 2017 declined slightly. *NSF.* Available from: https://www.nsf.gov/news/news_summ.jsp?cntn_id=297405

Networked Digital Library of Theses and Dissertations (NDLTD). (2020). Available from: http://www.ndltd.org/about

O'Shaughnessy, L. (July 2012). 12 reasons not to get a PhD. *CBS Moneywatch.* Available from: https://www.cbsnews.com/news/12-reasons-not-to-get-a-phd/

OECD. (2020). *Resourcing Higher Education: Challenges, Choices and Consequences. Higher Education*, Paris: OECD Publishing. Available from: DOI: 10.1787/735e1f44-en

Office for National Statistics (UK). (2018). *Estimating suicide among higher education students, England and Wales: experimental statistics.* Available from: https://www.ons.gov.uk/peoplepopulationandcommunity/birthsdeathsandmarriages/deaths/articles/estimatingsuicideamonghighereducationstudentsenglandandwalesexperimentalstatistics/2018-06-25

Ontario Human Rights Commission (OHRC). (2020). *Post-secondary education.* Available from: http://www.ohrc.on.ca/en/opportunity-succeed-achieving-barrier-free-education-students-disabilities/post-secondary-education

Open Access Theses and Dissertations. (2020). Available from: https://oatd.org/

Open Education Database. (2020). *Online PhD programs.* Available from: https://oedb.org/rankings/online-phd-programs/

Pearson PTE. (2020). *Unbiased English testing for study abroad and immigration.* Available from: https://pearsonpte.com/

PhD Stipends. (2020). *PhD stipend survey results.* Available from: http://www.phdstipends.com/results

ProQuest (PQDT). (2020). Available from: https://search.proquest.com/index?selectids=pqdt

QS World University Rankings. (2019). *Top universities.* Available from: https://www.topuniversities.com/university-rankings/world-university-rankings/2019

Shackle, S. (September 2019). 'The way universities are run is making us ill': inside the student mental health crisis. *The Guardian.* Available from: https://www.theguardian.com/society/2019/sep/27/anxiety-mental-breakdowns-depression-uk-students

Sowell, R. (2008). *PhD completion and attrition: analysis of baseline data.* Washington, DC: Council of Graduate Schools, 1–23. Available from: https://cgsnet.org/sites/default/files/phd_completion_attrition_baseline_program_data.pdf

Statistics Canada. (2020). *Labour force survey.* Available from: https://www150.statcan.gc.ca/n1/en/surveys/3701

The Cheeky Scientist. (2018). *The truth about PhD unemployment data.* Available from: https://www.youtube.com/watch?v=Ftma2Nd3zkQ

The Royal Society. (2010). *The scientific century: securing our future prosperity.* The Royal Society. Available from: https://royalsociety.org/~/media/Royal_Society_Content/policy/publications/2010/4294970126.pdf

Times Higher Education. (2020). *World university rankings.* Available from: https://www.timeshighereducation.com/world-university-rankings

Universities Australia. (2018). *2017 Universities Australia finances survey.* Available from: https://www.universitiesaustralia.edu.au/wp-content/uploads/2019/06/180713-2017-UA-Student-Finance-Survey-Report.pdf

Universities Australia. (2019). Higher education: facts and figures. Available from: https://www.universitiesaustralia.edu.au/wp-content/uploads/2019/08/190716-Facts-and-Figures-2019-Final-v2.pdf

University and College Union. (2020). *Second class academic citizens: the dehumanising effects of casualisation in higher education.* Available from: https://www.ucu.org.uk/media/10681/second_class_academic_citizens/pdf/secondclassacademiccitizens

University of Manchester. (2020). *Academic phrasebank.* Available from: http://www.phrasebank.manchester.ac.uk/

US Census Bureau. (2019). *Number of people with master's and doctoral degrees doubles since 2000. US Census Bureau (Education).* Available from: https://www.census.gov/library/stories/2019/02/number-of-people-with-masters-and-phd-degrees-double-since-2000.html

Vitae. (2020). *Employment levels for UK doctoral graduates.* Available from: https://www.vitae.ac.uk/doing-research/are-you-thinking-of-doing-a-phd/why-do-a-doctoral-degree/employment-levels-for-uk-doctoral-graduates

Webometrics Ranking of World Universities. (2020). *Universities: January 2020 Edition 2020.1.2 updated [Spanish language version also available].* Available from: http://webometrics.info/en/world

Which?. (2020). *University and student finance.* Available from: https://university.which.co.uk/advice/student-finance/how-much-debt-will-i-actually-get-into-by-going-to-university

Wikipedia. (2020). *Outline of academic disciplines.* Available from: https://en.wikipedia.org/wiki/Outline_of_academic_disciplines

Woolston, C. (December 2018). Why a postdoc might not advance your career. *Nature* [online]. Available from: https://www.nature.com/articles/d41586-018-07652-y

Woolston, C. (November 2019). PhDs: the tortuous truth. *Nature* [Online]. Available from: https://www.nature.com/articles/d41586-019-03459-7

Index

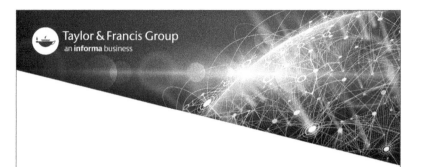

Lightning Source UK Ltd.
Milton Keynes UK
UKHW022041010822
406705UK00011B/250

9 780367 677640